THE FORBIDDEN
SECRET OF HUMANITY

Georges Simenon

INTRODUCTION

"The most beautiful experience we can have is the mysterious. It is the fundamental emotion that stands at the cradle of true art and true science."
Albert Einstein

The world around us is a tapestry woven with threads of mystery, intrigue, and untold secrets. From the enigmatic structures of ancient civilizations to the perplexing phenomena that defy our understanding, humanity has always been surrounded by the unknown. Yet, in the age of information, where answers are but a click away, we often find ourselves lulled into a false sense of comprehension, believing that the world has surrendered all its secrets to us.

But what if the most profound truths remain hidden, veiled by time, obscured by dogma, or simply overlooked in our relentless pursuit of progress? What if the legends whispered in hushed tones, the myths passed down through generations, and the anomalies dismissed by mainstream thought hold the keys to understanding our past, shaping our present, and illuminating our future?

Welcome to **"Forbidden Secrets of Humanity,"** a journey that transcends the boundaries of conventional wisdom and ventures into the realms of the unexplored. This book is not merely a collection of intriguing tales and speculative theories; it is an invitation to open your mind, challenge your perceptions, and embark on an odyssey that delves deep into the heart of human existence.

The Call to Adventure

Imagine standing at the edge of a vast ocean, the horizon stretching infinitely before you. Beneath the surface lies a world teeming with life, beauty, and secrets waiting to be discovered. To explore it requires courage, curiosity, and a willingness to dive into the depths, leaving the safety of the shore behind.

In the same way, **"Forbidden Secrets of Humanity"** beckons you to dive beneath the surface of accepted narratives and explore the depths of hidden knowledge. It is a call to question the stories we've been told, to seek the truths that lie beyond the veil, and to rediscover the wonders that have been forgotten or suppressed.

Unveiling the Hidden Layers

Throughout this journey, we will traverse time and space, exploring:

- **Lost Civilizations**: Uncovering evidence of advanced societies like Atlantis and Lemuria, whose legacies challenge our understanding of history.
- **Anomalies in Evolution**: Investigating the mysteries surrounding human origins and the potential existence of unknown hominid species.
- **Secret Societies**: Peering into the shadows cast by organizations like the Illuminati and Freemasons, and examining their influence on world events.
- **Esoteric Knowledge**: Decoding symbols, sacred geometry, and the hidden language that connects us to the cosmos.
- **Quantum Mysteries**: Bridging the gap between science and spirituality, and exploring how consciousness shapes reality.
- **Human Potential**: Unlocking the latent abilities within

us, from psychic phenomena to collective consciousness.

A Personal Journey

As you turn each page, you may find that this exploration becomes more than an intellectual pursuit; it becomes a personal journey of discovery. You may begin to see patterns where none were apparent before, feel a deeper connection to the world around you, and awaken aspects of yourself that have long been dormant.

Consider the story of **Dr. Elena Ramirez**, a marine archaeologist driven by a relentless quest to find the lost city of Atlantis. Her journey is not just about uncovering an ancient city but about challenging the limitations imposed by conventional science and daring to believe in possibilities beyond accepted norms.

Or reflect on **Amelia Hartwood**, the investigative journalist who delves into the enigmatic world of secret societies. Her pursuit of truth leads her down paths fraught with danger and deception, yet her unwavering determination illuminates the hidden forces shaping our reality.

These narratives, woven throughout the book, serve as both inspiration and reflection mirroring our own desires to seek, understand, and transcend.

Embracing the Unknown

It is important to approach this journey with both an open mind and a discerning eye. The topics explored are complex, often controversial, and sometimes speculative. They exist at the intersection of fact and fiction, science and mysticism, reality and imagination.

Yet, it is within this intersection that innovation thrives, where breakthroughs occur, and where humanity has historically leaped forward. The courage to explore the unknown has led to the greatest discoveries and the most profound advancements.

The Invitation

I invite you to step into the unknown, to walk paths less traveled, and to embrace the mysteries that have both confounded and captivated humanity since the dawn of time.

As you embark on this journey through **"Forbidden Secrets of Humanity,"** remember that every great adventure begins with a single step into the unexplored. Let this book be your compass, guiding you through the labyrinth of secrets and illuminating the shadows with the light of knowledge.

Are you ready to discover the forbidden secrets that could change everything?

PART I: THE MYSTERIOUS ORIGINS OF HUMANITY

CHAPTER 1: LOST CIVILIZATIONS AND FORGOTTEN LEGENDS UNCOVERING EVIDENCE OF ADVANCED SOCIETIES LIKE ATLANTIS AND LEMURIA

"Lost civilizations are more than myths; they are the echoes of forgotten societies whose legacies challenge the very foundations of history."

Dr. Alexander Marlowe

Prologue

The idea of lost civilizations has captivated human imagination for centuries. From the submerged continent of Atlantis to the sunken lands of Lemuria, these ancient societies have been the subject of countless myths, legends, and speculative theories. Were they advanced cultures with knowledge and technologies that rival or surpass our own? Or are they simply allegorical tales meant to teach moral lessons? In his study filled with ancient maps, weathered manuscripts, and archeological reports, Dr. Alexander Marlowe embarks on a journey to uncover the truth behind these enigmatic civilizations. As he sifts through evidence, he finds clues that suggest these lost societies were not just products of legend but potentially real cultures that wielded extraordinary knowledge, forever altering our understanding of human history.

Atlantis: The Fabled Island of Advanced Technology and Knowledge

The story of Atlantis originates from the writings of the Greek philosopher Plato, who described it as a powerful and advanced civilization that existed around 9,000 years before his time. According to Plato, Atlantis was a highly developed society with impressive architecture, advanced technology, and a profound understanding of mathematics and science. Yet, it was also a civilization marked by moral decay, which ultimately led to its destruction by a catastrophic event that submerged it beneath the ocean.

The Historical and Philosophical Context

- **Plato's Dialogues**: Atlantis is introduced in Plato's works "Timaeus" and "Critias." He describes the Atlanteans as possessing vast wealth, sophisticated urban planning, and technological prowess that allowed them to dominate surrounding regions.

- **Possible Inspirations**: Some historians believe Plato's account may have been inspired by real-world events, such as the destruction of the Minoan civilization on the island of Crete due to a massive volcanic eruption around 1600 BCE. However, others argue that Atlantis was purely allegorical, serving as a cautionary tale about hubris and the moral downfall of a powerful empire.

Advanced Engineering and Urban Planning

- **Architectural Marvels**: According to Plato, Atlantis was structured in a series of concentric rings of water and land, with the central island housing the grand capital. The city featured advanced architecture, including massive temples, grand canals, and sophisticated bridges. This description suggests a level of urban planning and engineering that surpasses known ancient cultures.

- **Technological Mastery**: Accounts hint that Atlanteans may have had access to technologies far ahead of their time, such as hydraulic systems, advanced metallurgy, and potentially even forms of energy generation unknown to other contemporary civilizations.

Potential Archaeological Evidence

- **The Bimini Road**: Off the coast of Bimini in the Bahamas, divers discovered an underwater rock formation resembling a paved road, known as the Bimini Road. Some theorists argue this could be remnants of Atlantean architecture, though mainstream archaeology considers it a natural formation.

- **Santorini and the Minoan Connection**: The volcanic eruption of Santorini is often linked to the possible destruction of a real-life Atlantis. The eruption devastated the Minoan civilization, which boasted advanced maritime trade, complex architecture, and sophisticated artwork that echo aspects of Plato's Atlantis.

- **The Richat Structure (Eye of the Sahara)**: Located in Mauritania, the Richat Structure bears a striking resemblance to Plato's description of Atlantis. This geological formation features circular rings that some believe align with the Atlantean city's layout. Though debated, it has fueled speculation that Atlantis could have been located in this part of Africa.

Theories of Advanced Atlantean Technology

- **Crystal Energy and Power Sources**: Some speculative theories suggest that Atlanteans utilized crystal energy or other advanced power sources, harnessing natural energy fields. These ideas, while lacking concrete evidence, align with the concept of a civilization with superior technological capabilities that could influence natural forces in ways that seem almost magical.

- **Anti-Gravity and Aerial Navigation**: Myths around Atlantis occasionally reference technologies that resemble flying machines or anti-gravity devices. While these claims are largely dismissed by mainstream historians, they continue to capture the imagination of those who believe in ancient advanced technologies.

Lemuria: The Lost Continent of Spiritual Wisdom and Ancient Knowledge

Lemuria, often linked with the mystical concept of Mu, is another lost civilization said to have existed in the Indian or Pacific Ocean. Unlike the technological grandeur of Atlantis, Lemuria is often depicted as a spiritually advanced society, emphasizing harmony with nature, deep metaphysical wisdom, and advanced forms of communication.

Origins and Theories

- **Theosophical Connections**: The concept of Lemuria was popularized in the late 19th century by Helena Blavatsky and the Theosophical Society, who claimed that Lemuria was home to an ancient, spiritually evolved race of people. These beings were said to possess psychic abilities, deep esoteric knowledge, and a profound connection to the earth's energy.

- **Scientific Speculations**: Initially, some scientists proposed Lemuria to explain similarities in flora and fauna between India, Africa, and Madagascar. However, the theory was largely abandoned in favor of plate tectonics, which provided a more accurate explanation of continental drift.

Cultural and Spiritual Attributes

- **Advanced Spirituality and Healing**: Lemuria is often portrayed as a civilization that mastered healing arts, energy manipulation, and holistic practices that promoted longevity and spiritual enlightenment. It's believed that the Lemurians had a deep understanding of plant medicine, crystal healing, and vibrational energy techniques that far surpassed those known in later civilizations.

- **Telepathy and Advanced Communication**: Myths suggest that Lemurians communicated telepathically and were able to access higher dimensions of consciousness. Their society was built on principles of peace, cooperation, and mutual respect, unlike the more hierarchical and warlike structures often attributed to Atlantis.

Possible Remnants and Evidence

- **Sunken Temples and Ruins**: Off the coast of

India and Japan, there are submerged structures, such as the underwater ruins near Yonaguni Island, that some speculate could be remnants of Lemurian architecture. Though most archaeologists attribute these formations to natural causes, they remain a point of intrigue for those who believe in the existence of ancient sunken cities.

- **Kumari Kandam and Tamil Legends**: In South Indian tradition, the lost land of Kumari Kandam is believed to have sunk beneath the Indian Ocean. Tamil legends describe it as a highly advanced civilization that predates recorded history, with sophisticated knowledge of mathematics, astronomy, and philosophy.

- **Crystal Skulls and Lemurian Legacy**: Certain new-age beliefs link the enigmatic crystal skulls found in various locations around the world to Lemuria, suggesting they are ancient artifacts containing encoded knowledge from this lost civilization.

Theoretical Technologies and Knowledge

- **Vril Energy and Life Force Manipulation**: Lemuria is often associated with the concept of Vril or prana universal life force energy that could be harnessed for healing, communication, and even materialization of objects. While speculative, this aligns with ancient practices that emphasize energy work, similar to Reiki and other modern spiritual healing techniques.

- **Atlantis vs. Lemuria**: Although Atlantis and Lemuria are often compared, they represent contrasting archetypes. Atlantis symbolizes technological prowess and human ambition, while Lemuria embodies spiritual wisdom and a harmonious way of life. Some theories propose that conflict between the two led to their mutual destruction, representing a broader allegory of the balance between material and spiritual pursuits.

The Implications of Lost Civilizations

Rewriting Human History

- **Challenging the Timeline**: Discoveries hinting at lost civilizations like Atlantis and Lemuria force a reevaluation of humanity's historical timeline. Evidence of advanced societies predating known ancient cultures suggests that human civilization's rise may have occurred far earlier and with greater complexity than previously acknowledged.

- **Hidden Knowledge**: If these civilizations existed, they may have possessed advanced knowledge and technologies that were lost with their demise. The potential recovery of such knowledge could have profound implications for modern society, from understanding energy systems to redefining our spiritual and philosophical perspectives.

Advanced Technologies and Spiritual Practice

- **Technological Parallels**: The engineering feats attributed to Atlantis and Lemuria resonate with modern technologies such as renewable energy, holistic medicine, and advanced communication systems. Exploring these parallels may inspire innovations grounded in ancient wisdom.

- **Spiritual Resurgence**: The renewed interest in the spiritual practices of lost civilizations reflects a contemporary desire to reconnect with more holistic ways of living. Practices such as meditation, energy healing, and sustainable living are reminiscent of Lemurian teachings, suggesting a revival of ancient wisdom in the modern age.

Modern Explorations and Theories

- **Underwater Archeology**: Advances in underwater archeology and remote sensing technology continue to reveal submerged structures that may provide clues to lost civilizations. As technology improves, the potential to uncover definitive evidence of these advanced societies grows, offering the promise of new historical narratives.

- **Mysticism and New-Age Beliefs**: The enduring fascination with Atlantis and Lemuria fuels a wide range of new-age beliefs and spiritual movements. While these perspectives often blend mythology with speculative science, they reflect a deeper yearning to understand humanity's origins and potential.

Case Study: The Mystery of the Yonaguni Monument A Glimpse into a Sunken World

Discovered off the coast of Japan, the Yonaguni Monument is an underwater rock formation that has sparked debates over its origins. Resembling a series of terraces, platforms, and stone blocks, it raises the question: Is it a natural geological formation, or could it be evidence of a long-lost civilization, possibly Lemurian?

Research Methodology

Geological and Structural Analysis

- **Terrace and Platform Examination**: Geologists have analyzed the formation, noting sharp edges and right angles that appear unnatural. Some suggest that this could be evidence of human modification, while others argue these features are the result of natural erosion.

- **Carvings and Potential Hieroglyphs**: Divers have reported discovering what appear to be carvings and hieroglyphs on the stone surfaces, though these claims are widely debated and require further validation.

Symbolic and Cultural Significance

- **Comparison to Other Ancient Sites**: The monument's features have been compared to other ancient megalithic sites, including those in South America and Easter Island, suggesting possible cultural connections or shared architectural knowledge.

- **Speculative Links to Lemuria**: Proponents of the Lemurian theory argue that the monument's underwater location aligns with myths of a sunken civilization in the Pacific, reinforcing narratives of a great ancient culture lost to cataclysm.

Implications for Historical Understanding

- **If Proven Artificial**: Should the monument be proven to be man-made, it would suggest the presence of a sophisticated society capable of large-scale stonework during a time period when such achievements are not believed to have existed in the region.

- **Cultural Legacy**: Whether natural or artificial, the site continues to capture imaginations and fuel the ongoing debate about lost civilizations, serving as a powerful symbol of humanity's enduring quest to uncover the secrets of our past.

Conclusion

The legends of Atlantis and Lemuria are more than mere stories they are windows into humanity's collective memory, hinting at civilizations that may have thrived long before recorded history began. Whether purely mythological or based in truth, these lost societies challenge us to reconsider the boundaries of human potential. As new evidence emerges from the depths of the ocean and the sands of time, the line between myth and history grows ever thinner, inviting us to explore the forgotten chapters of our past. In doing so, we may not only rediscover ancient knowledge but also reclaim a part of ourselves that has long been lost to the waves.

"The search for lost civilizations is not just about uncovering the past; it's about unlocking the mysteries of who we are and what we are capable of achieving."
Dr. Alexander Marlowe

Reflection Questions:

How do the accounts of Atlantis and Lemuria influence our understanding of human history and technological development? What lessons can modern society learn from these ancient narratives?

What are the implications of discovering evidence of advanced lost civilizations for our current scientific and historical paradigms? How might this change our approach to studying ancient cultures?

How do myths of lost civilizations reflect humanity's ongoing quest for knowledge, and why do these stories

continue to resonate so powerfully in our collective imagination?

CHAPTER 2: GÖBEKLI TEPE AND PREHISTORIC MYSTERIES CHALLENGING THE OFFICIAL CHRONOLOGY OF HUMAN HISTORY

"Göbekli Tepe is not just a site; it's a revelation that forces us to rethink the origins of civilization itself."
Dr. Lena Richter

Prologue

High on a hilltop in southeastern Turkey, the ancient site of Göbekli Tepe has redefined everything we thought we knew about the dawn of human civilization. Discovered in the 1960s and only excavated in earnest beginning in the 1990s, this prehistoric complex, estimated to be over 12,000 years old, predates Stonehenge and the Great Pyramids of Giza by several millennia. With its massive stone pillars arranged in circles and adorned with intricate carvings of animals, Göbekli Tepe challenges the traditional narrative that agriculture preceded the rise of complex societies and monumental architecture. Instead, this site suggests that the desire to worship, connect, and create may have been the true catalyst for civilization. As Dr. Lena Richter walks among the towering stones, she contemplates the mysterious people who built this site long before the advent of writing, pottery, or the wheel. What secrets did they hold, and why did they bury this grand monument, only to leave it hidden for thousands of years?

Göbekli Tepe: The World's Oldest Temple?

Göbekli Tepe is often referred to as the world's oldest known temple. Its discovery has upended traditional views of prehistory, revealing a sophisticated society capable of organizing, constructing, and possibly even performing complex rituals long before the advent of settled farming communities.

Discovery and Early Excavations

- **Initial Findings**: Although discovered in the 1960s, the site did not gain significant attention until German archaeologist Klaus Schmidt began excavations in the

1990s. What he uncovered stunned the archaeological world: massive stone circles, expertly carved and carefully positioned, that were built by hunter-gatherers.

- **Age and Significance**: Radiocarbon dating places the site at around 9600 BCE, making it approximately 12,000 years old. This period, known as the Pre-Pottery Neolithic, predates the advent of agriculture by thousands of years, suggesting that organized religion and communal rituals may have been the driving forces behind early societal development.

- **Burial of the Site**: Unusually, Göbekli Tepe was deliberately buried by its creators around 8,000 BCE. The reasons for this are still unknown, but theories range from ritualistic purposes to a desire to preserve their legacy. The deliberate backfilling has also preserved the site in exceptional condition, offering a unique window into the past.

Architectural and Artistic Features

- **Massive Stone Pillars**: The site features numerous T-shaped limestone pillars, some weighing up to 20 tons and reaching heights of over 5 meters. These pillars are arranged in circular enclosures and often display elaborate carvings of animals such as lions, snakes, boars, and birds.

- **Intricate Reliefs and Symbols**: The carvings on the pillars are not mere decorations; they are thought to hold symbolic or spiritual significance. The presence of animals, abstract symbols, and humanoid figures suggests that the site was used for complex ritualistic practices, possibly connected to a belief system that predated formal religion.

- **Construction Techniques**: The builders of Göbekli Tepe possessed advanced knowledge of stone working, as evidenced by the precision of the carvings and the construction of the enclosures. Despite lacking metal tools, they managed to quarry, transport, and erect these massive stones using techniques that remain a subject of ongoing research.

Implications for Understanding Human Society

- **Challenging the Agricultural Hypothesis**: Prior to the discovery of Göbekli Tepe, it was widely believed that the development of agriculture was the primary catalyst for the rise of complex societies and monumental architecture. Göbekli Tepe, however, predates the widespread domestication of plants and animals, suggesting that social and religious structures may have been established before agricultural settlements.

- **Social Organization**: The scale of construction indicates that large groups of people had to work together over extended periods, implying a level of social organization and cooperation that was previously not attributed to hunter-gatherer groups. This challenges the notion that complex social hierarchies only emerged with settled farming.

- **Ritual and Religion as Catalysts**: The evidence suggests that the desire to gather for ritualistic purposes perhaps to honor gods, ancestors, or celestial events may have been a driving force in human societal evolution. This perspective emphasizes the importance of symbolic thinking, spiritual beliefs, and communal activities in shaping early human culture.

Other Prehistoric Sites That Challenge the Timeline

Göbekli Tepe is not alone in its mystery. Other prehistoric sites around the world also defy conventional historical narratives, hinting at a global web of early human ingenuity that has yet to be fully understood.

Çatalhöyük: The Urban Pioneer

- **Location and Age**: Located in modern-day Turkey, Çatalhöyük is one of the earliest known urban centers, dating back to approximately 7500 BCE. Unlike Göbekli Tepe, Çatalhöyük was a fully developed city with homes, communal areas, and evidence of a sedentary lifestyle.

- **Unique Architecture**: The city was built without streets; houses were clustered together with entry through the roofs, suggesting a highly organized and cooperative society. The interiors were richly decorated with murals, figurines, and symbols, reflecting a complex spiritual life.

- **Agriculture and Trade**: Unlike Göbekli Tepe, Çatalhöyük was an agricultural society, growing crops and raising animals. Its location along trade routes facilitated the exchange of goods, ideas, and cultural practices, making it a hub of early civilization.

The Hypogeum of Hal-Saflieni: Malta's Underground Temple

- **Location and Description**: The Hypogeum is a subterranean structure on the island of Malta, believed to date back to around 4000 BCE. This underground temple and burial site was carved entirely out of rock, featuring chambers, altars, and a unique acoustic phenomenon in its main hall.

- **Ritual Significance**: The Hypogeum is believed to have been a place of worship and burial, reflecting advanced spiritual and architectural knowledge. The acoustic properties of the space suggest it was used for chanting or other sound-based rituals, enhancing the spiritual experience.

- **Artistic Mastery**: The walls are adorned with intricate carvings and red ochre paintings, depicting spirals, animals, and abstract patterns. The level of artistic sophistication indicates a society deeply connected to symbolic representation and ritual practice.

Stonehenge: The Astronomical Enigma

- **Location and Age**: Located in Wiltshire, England, Stonehenge was constructed between 3000 BCE and 2000 BCE. Although much younger than Göbekli Tepe, it shares the theme of monumental architecture built for ritualistic or astronomical purposes.

- **Astronomical Alignments**: Stonehenge is famously aligned with the solstices, suggesting it functioned as a solar calendar or a site for celestial worship. This alignment with the sun's movements indicates an advanced understanding of astronomy.

- **Construction Mysteries**: The transportation of the massive sarsen stones, some weighing up to 30 tons, remains one of the great engineering puzzles of prehistory. Theories range from sledges and rollers to elaborate pulley systems, but the exact methods are still debated.

Theories of Advanced Ancestral Civilizations

The existence of sites like Göbekli Tepe, Çatalhöyük, the Hypogeum, and Stonehenge has led some researchers to speculate that prehistoric humanity possessed a more advanced level of knowledge than previously believed. These theories challenge the traditional linear progression of human development.

Ancient Knowledge and Lost Technologies

- **Stone-Carving Techniques**: The precision and scale of stone carving at sites like Göbekli Tepe suggest a mastery of techniques that are not well understood. Some theorists propose that ancient civilizations might have developed lost technologies or tools that enabled them to achieve such feats.

- **Geometrical and Mathematical Skills**: Many prehistoric structures exhibit precise geometrical alignments and proportions, indicating a sophisticated understanding of mathematics. This challenges the notion that advanced mathematical concepts only emerged with later civilizations like the Greeks or Egyptians.

- **Prehistoric Astronomy**: The alignment of ancient sites with celestial bodies suggests that early humans had a profound understanding of the stars and their movements. This knowledge may have been passed down through oral traditions, encoded in monuments, or linked to ritualistic practices that connected the earthly with the divine.

Global Connections and Shared Knowledge

- **Cultural Parallels**: Similar architectural styles, symbolic motifs, and construction techniques found in diverse regions of the world suggest the possibility of cultural diffusion or shared knowledge among prehistoric societies. This could imply a more interconnected ancient world than previously thought.

- **Advanced Navigation and Trade**: Evidence of long-distance trade routes and the movement of materials like obsidian, copper, and exotic stones supports the idea that early humans were capable of complex logistics and navigation. This suggests that prehistoric societies were not isolated but engaged in significant cultural exchange.

Catastrophic Events and the Loss of Knowledge

- **Younger Dryas Impact Hypothesis**: Some researchers propose that a catastrophic event, such as a comet impact during the Younger Dryas period (around 12,800 years ago), could have led to the sudden decline of advanced prehistoric societies. Such an event would have caused widespread environmental changes, disrupting early human settlements and leading to the loss of accumulated knowledge.

- **Great Flood Myths**: Legends of great floods found in cultures worldwide, from the Biblical Noah to the Mesopotamian Gilgamesh, suggest that ancient societies may have experienced cataclysmic events that wiped out entire civilizations. These stories could be remnants of collective memories of real prehistoric disasters that reset the clock on human progress.

Implications for Modern Understanding

Rewriting the Narrative of Civilization

- **Rethinking Progress**: The discoveries at Göbekli Tepe and other prehistoric sites challenge the conventional narrative that human progress followed a straightforward path from hunter-gatherers to complex societies. Instead, these sites suggest that early humans were capable of remarkable achievements long before the rise of cities and states.

- **Spirituality and Society**: The importance of ritual, symbolism, and communal gathering in early human societies underscores the role of spirituality as a foundational element of civilization. This challenges the often secular view of societal development and highlights the interplay between belief and community.

Rediscovering Ancient Wisdom

- **Inspiration for Modern Architecture and Engineering**: The precision and ingenuity displayed at sites like Göbekli Tepe can inspire contemporary architecture and engineering, emphasizing the importance of working with natural materials, understanding environmental contexts, and incorporating symbolic elements.

- **Learning from Prehistoric Sustainability**: Prehistoric societies often lived in harmony with their environments, utilizing local resources and sustainable practices. Modern societies can learn from these ancient models to address current challenges related to environmental degradation and resource management.

The Ongoing Quest for Humanity's Origins

- **Continued Exploration**: As technology advances, new methods in archaeology, such as ground-penetrating radar, satellite imaging, and advanced dating techniques, will continue to reveal hidden structures and unknown aspects of prehistoric life. These discoveries have the potential to reshape our understanding of where we come from and how our ancestors lived.

- **Cultural and Philosophical Reflections**: The revelations of prehistoric monuments invite us to reflect on the deeper aspects of human existence our need to create, to connect, and to understand the world around us. By exploring these ancient mysteries, we gain not just knowledge but a renewed appreciation for the enduring human spirit.

Conclusion

Göbekli Tepe and other prehistoric sites offer a tantalizing glimpse into a forgotten chapter of human history, one that defies easy explanations and challenges our assumptions about the origins of civilization. These ancient structures, built with astonishing skill and purpose, remind us that humanity's journey is far more complex and mysterious than previously thought. As we continue to explore and uncover the secrets of these enigmatic places, we are reminded that the past holds not just answers but also profound questions about who we are and what we are capable of achieving.

"Prehistoric monuments are messages from our ancestors, carved in stone, speaking to us across millennia. They tell us that even in the earliest days of human history, we were already reaching for the stars."
Dr. Lena Richter

Reflection Questions:

> **How do the discoveries at Göbekli Tepe challenge our current understanding of the origins of civilization? What does this site tell us about the role of spirituality and communal activities in early human societies?**

> **What implications do the alignments of prehistoric structures with celestial bodies have for our understanding of ancient knowledge and technology? How might this knowledge have influenced the development of early cultures?**

> **Why do you think prehistoric societies were capable of constructing such advanced structures, and what might have led to the loss of this knowledge over time? How can modern research help us recover and learn from these ancient achievements?**

CHAPTER 3: THEORIES OF ADVANCED ANCESTRAL CIVILIZATIONS EXPLORING HUMANITY'S FORGOTTEN TECHNOLOGICAL HEIGHTS

"History, as we know it, is only a faint whisper of a much older story a story that suggests our ancestors may have reached technological and intellectual heights far beyond

what we ever imagined."
Dr. Marcus Valente

Prologue

From the awe-inspiring precision of ancient monuments to the inexplicable artifacts that defy historical timelines, there is growing evidence that our ancestors may have possessed technologies and knowledge that rival or even surpass modern capabilities. These are not just fringe theories but are increasingly supported by compelling finds that challenge the orthodox view of human development. As Dr. Marcus Valente pours over ancient texts, advanced archaeological models, and unclassified historical records, he finds himself drawn into a narrative that suggests human civilization may have once reached remarkable technological heights, only to be lost to time. This chapter delves into the possibility that humanity's past is not one of simple progression from primitive to advanced, but rather a series of peaks and valleys periods of incredible achievement followed by catastrophic losses. What remains hidden in these lost chapters of human history? And what can we learn from the echoes of our advanced ancestors?

Evidence of Advanced Ancestral Civilizations

From ancient megalithic structures that defy modern construction techniques to mysterious artifacts with unknown purposes, the physical evidence left behind by these potential lost civilizations continues to baffle and inspire researchers.

Impossible Megaliths and Mysterious Monuments

- **Ba'albek, Lebanon**: Home to the massive Temple of Jupiter, Ba'albek features some of the largest cut stones in the world, including the Stone of the Pregnant Woman, weighing an estimated 1,200 tons. How these stones were transported and lifted into place remains a mystery that challenges even modern engineering capabilities. Some theories suggest the use of advanced machinery or forgotten technologies far beyond the known tools of the time.

- **The Pyramids of Giza**: While the Great Pyramid of Giza is well-known, its construction continues to pose questions. With blocks weighing up to 80 tons transported from quarries miles away, the precision alignment to true north, and the complex internal structures, some speculate that the builders had access to advanced engineering knowledge, possibly involving levitation or energy manipulation technologies that are now lost.

- **Puma Punku, Bolivia**: Part of the Tiwanaku complex, Puma Punku is renowned for its precisely cut andesite blocks, some weighing several tons and intricately carved with perfect interlocking notches. The precision of these cuts, which seem to require machine-like tools, defies explanation considering the lack of metal tools among the known technologies of the time. The exact purpose and methods behind these constructions remain speculative.

Ancient Artifacts with Unknown Purposes

- **The Antikythera Mechanism**: Discovered in a shipwreck off the coast of Greece, this complex device dates back to around 100 BCE and is often described as the world's first analog computer. It was used to predict astronomical positions and eclipses with astonishing accuracy. The mechanism's intricate gears and precise craftsmanship suggest that ancient civilizations possessed far more advanced technological capabilities than previously recognized.

- **The Baghdad Battery**: This set of artifacts, found near Baghdad and dating back to the Parthian period (roughly 250 BCE), appears to be an early form of a galvanic cell, or battery. Composed of a clay jar, copper cylinder, and iron rod, it suggests that ancient peoples may have known how to generate electricity long before the modern era, possibly using it for electroplating or medical treatments.

- **The Sabu Disc**: Found in the tomb of Prince Sabu in Egypt, this enigmatic object resembles a stone wheel with an unknown function. Dating back to around 3000 BCE, its precise shape and intricate design have led some to speculate it was part of an unknown mechanical device, a water pump, or even a component of an ancient energy system.

Prehistoric Maps and Advanced Cartography

- **The Piri Reis Map**: This 16th-century map, drawn by the Ottoman admiral Piri Reis, depicts the coastlines of South America and Antarctica with remarkable accuracy, including details of the Antarctic coast free of ice an image that should not have been possible without aerial or satellite surveying technology. Some researchers suggest that the map could be based on ancient sources from a lost civilization with advanced mapping skills.

- **The Map of the Creator**: Discovered in Russia, this stone slab features an intricate 3D topographical map of the Ural Mountains, complete with a system of canals, dams, and civil engineering projects. Dated at over 100 million years old, according to some controversial studies, it challenges everything we know about the history of cartography and the capabilities of ancient humans.

Sacred Geometry and Advanced Mathematical Knowledge

- **Ancient Mathematics**: Many ancient structures exhibit precise mathematical constants, such as the golden ratio and pi, suggesting that early civilizations possessed advanced mathematical knowledge. This is evident in the design of the Great Pyramid, the layout of Teotihuacan, and the intricate patterns found in Hindu and Buddhist temples.

- **Geometric Alignment of Monuments**: A growing body of evidence suggests that ancient sites across the globe, from Stonehenge to the Nazca Lines, are aligned according to specific geometric patterns and ley lines. These alignments often correspond to celestial events, indicating a deep understanding of both terrestrial and astronomical knowledge.

Theories of Lost Technologies and Advanced Knowledge

The artifacts and monuments left behind suggest that ancient civilizations may have harnessed technologies and scientific knowledge that are either lost or still not understood by modern science. Below are some of the most compelling theories.

Energy Manipulation and Unknown Power Sources

- **Wireless Energy Transmission**: Inspired by the work of Nikola Tesla, some theorists suggest that ancient civilizations could have developed methods to transmit energy wirelessly. The pyramids, obelisks, and other towering structures might have acted as conductors or resonators of energy, harnessing the Earth's natural electromagnetic field. This theory aligns with tales of ancient power sources, like the Ark of the Covenant, which is described in biblical texts as emitting dangerous energy.

- **Piezoelectricity and Stone**: Certain ancient structures, including those built from quartz-rich stones, might have been designed to harness piezoelectric effects, converting mechanical stress into electrical energy. This theory posits that the builders could have used this energy for unknown technological or ritualistic purposes.

- **Sound Levitation**: Some believe that ancient peoples used acoustic technology specific frequencies and sound waves to lift and move massive stones. Legends from Tibet, Egypt, and South America mention the use of sound in construction, such as the myth of priests singing stones into place. While still speculative, experiments have shown that sound waves can indeed levitate small objects, suggesting that ancient knowledge of acoustics might have been far more advanced than we understand.

Advanced Metallurgy and Material Science

- **Orichalcum and Lost Alloys**: Ancient texts, including those describing Atlantis, reference metals and alloys that no longer exist today. Orichalcum, said to be a precious metal second only to gold, was recently discovered in shipwrecks off the coast of Sicily. Its precise composition and uses remain speculative, but its existence hints at lost metallurgical practices.

- **Vitrified Fortresses**: Scattered across Europe are ancient fortresses with walls that have been vitrified melted and fused through extreme heat. This phenomenon cannot be replicated easily, even with modern technology, and suggests that ancient peoples possessed advanced techniques for producing high temperatures, possibly involving unknown energy sources or chemical processes.

High-Precision Tools and Machinery

- **Ancient Machining Marks**: Many ancient structures, particularly in Egypt and South America, display cuts and drill holes that suggest the use of high-precision tools, possibly diamond-tipped or ultrasonic machinery. Such tools would be necessary to achieve the near-perfect smoothness and precision seen in stones at Puma Punku or the granite sarcophagi of the Serapeum in Saqqara.

- **Lost Engineering Blueprints**: Some speculate that these ancient technologies were documented in texts now lost or hidden, possibly within the fabled Library of Alexandria or secret chambers beneath the Sphinx. The possibility that blueprints for these advanced tools exist in hidden caches continues to fuel treasure hunts and conspiracy theories worldwide.

Implications of Advanced Ancestral Civilizations for Modern Society

If humanity once reached advanced technological and intellectual heights, only to be brought low by catastrophe, conflict, or time, it raises profound questions about our present trajectory and future potential.

Re-evaluating Human History

- **The Non-Linear Model of Civilization**: Traditional views of human history depict a steady, linear progression from primitive to advanced societies. However, the evidence of lost technologies suggests a more cyclical model, where peaks of human achievement are followed by collapses that reset the course of civilization. This paradigm shift encourages a re-examination of historical narratives and the recognition that human ingenuity has deep, ancient roots.

- **Rediscovering Lost Wisdom**: Modern technology has allowed us to achieve great advancements, but it also comes with environmental and social costs. Ancient societies often lived in harmony with nature, and studying their approaches to energy, agriculture, and medicine could offer sustainable solutions for today's challenges.

The Potential of Hidden Technologies

- **Reclaiming Ancient Energy Sources**: If technologies like wireless energy transmission, advanced metallurgy, and acoustic levitation existed in the past, their rediscovery could revolutionize our current energy and construction industries. This would not only reduce dependence on fossil fuels but also inspire new innovations grounded in ancient wisdom.

- **Medical and Healing Practices**: The healing techniques of lost civilizations, often dismissed as superstition, could hold keys to natural and holistic approaches that modern medicine overlooks. Research into plant medicine, sound therapy, and alternative healing methods rooted in ancient practices could unlock new frontiers in health care.

Preparing for the Future

- **Avoiding Past Mistakes**: Understanding the rise and fall of advanced ancestral civilizations can provide valuable lessons about the fragility of progress. Environmental degradation, social inequality, and the misuse of technology may have contributed to past collapses. Learning from these examples, we can strive to build a future that prioritizes sustainability, equity, and the responsible use of technology.

- **Embracing the Unknown**: The evidence of lost civilizations serves as a humbling reminder that there is still much we do not know about our past. As we continue to explore, dig deeper, and question established narratives, we are reminded to keep an open mind and embrace the possibility that human potential is far greater than we have yet realized.

Conclusion

Theories of advanced ancestral civilizations challenge the conventional understanding of human history, inviting us to reconsider what we know about the origins of technology, society, and intelligence. Whether through ancient megaliths, mysterious artifacts, or forgotten texts, the clues left behind by our ancestors hint at a world rich in knowledge and innovation. By exploring these hidden chapters of humanity's past, we not only honor those who came before us but also uncover the potential for a future where ancient wisdom and modern science converge.

"The lost technologies of our ancestors are not just relics of a forgotten past; they are beacons lighting the way to what we can achieve when we dare to dream beyond the boundaries of our present knowledge."
Dr. Marcus Valente

Reflection Questions:

> **What are the most compelling pieces of evidence that suggest ancient civilizations possessed advanced technologies? How do these findings challenge our current understanding of human history?**

> **How might the rediscovery of lost technologies and knowledge impact modern society, particularly in areas like energy, medicine, and architecture?**

> **Why do you think ancient societies may have lost their advanced technologies, and what lessons can we learn from their rise and fall as we look to the future?**

PERSONAL REFLECTIONS AND TESTIMONIES

A Researcher's Encounter with the Legacy of Atlantis

Dr. Adrian Rivera, an archaeologist specializing in ancient civilizations, shares his personal reflections on his groundbreaking discovery in the Azores an area many have long believed could be a remnant of the lost civilization of Atlantis:

"I've spent over twenty years studying the ruins and artifacts of ancient civilizations, but nothing prepared me for what I found in the Azores. At first glance, the ruins seemed similar to other Bronze Age sites, but there was something different, something more advanced. The craftsmanship, the layout of the structures, and the positioning of these ruins in relation to celestial bodies all hinted at an advanced knowledge of astronomy and geometry far beyond what should have been possible at the time.

While exploring one particular temple, I discovered an inscription in a language that didn't match any known ancient script. The symbols were strangely familiar, almost resonant, as though they belonged to a civilization I had studied my entire life but could never fully grasp. It reminded me of the descriptions of Atlantis an advanced civilization lost to history, but whose legacy lingers in myth.

I spent weeks trying to decipher the text, and although I didn't unlock its full meaning, I realized that this find could change everything we know about human history. Could these ruins be evidence of the Atlanteans or a precursor civilization with knowledge lost after a great cataclysm? As I stood before those inscriptions, I felt a deep connection to a past I had never imagined was possible. The idea that entire chapters of human history are missing, buried under centuries of forgetfulness, has transformed how I approach my work. I'm no longer just a seeker of artifacts; I am a seeker of forgotten truths."

A Spiritual Connection to Lemuria

Lara Moonflower, a spiritual healer, shares her experience of connecting with the energy of Lemuria, a lost civilization said to have thrived in the Pacific Ocean:

"I've always felt drawn to the ocean, but it wasn't until I

visited Hawaii that I truly understood why. One evening, while meditating by the shore, I had a profound experience. I saw images flash before my eyes tall, graceful beings standing among crystal structures, surrounded by lush, vibrant landscapes. They seemed peaceful and deeply connected to the Earth, to each other, and to a higher consciousness. I had no idea what these visions meant until a few days later, when I stumbled upon a book about Lemuria. The images matched exactly what I had seen in my meditation.

The energy I felt from that vision was unlike anything I had experienced before. It was as if the essence of Lemuria, a civilization believed to have lived in harmony with nature, was still alive in the Earth's energy field, waiting for us to reconnect with it. Since then, I have dedicated myself to working with the Earth's energies, helping people remember their connection to nature and to the ancient wisdom that is still accessible if we're willing to open ourselves to it. I truly believe that Lemuria and other forgotten civilizations hold the key to unlocking our future."

PRACTICAL APPLICATIONS AND ACTION STEPS

Unlocking the Mysteries of Lost Civilizations: Steps You Can Take

As we delve into the mysteries of lost civilizations like Atlantis and Lemuria, it's important to recognize that these forgotten cultures may hold the keys to understanding the full potential of humanity. Here are some practical ways you can explore and integrate the knowledge of these ancient civilizations into your life:

Study the Ancient Texts and Mythologies

- **Action Step**: Start by reading the ancient texts that mention lost civilizations, such as Plato's accounts of Atlantis or the Polynesian myths of Mu and Lemuria. These texts provide symbolic and historical clues about the wisdom of these civilizations.

- **Application**: Look for common themes spiritual advancement, harmony with nature, and the use of advanced technology that transcend culture and time. Reflect on how these themes can be applied to modern life.

Visit Sacred Sites and Meditate on Their Energy

- **Action Step**: If possible, visit sites believed to be remnants of these lost civilizations, such as the ruins in the Azores or underwater structures off the coast of Japan. If travel isn't an option, engage in virtual tours or research.

- **Application**: When at a sacred site (physically or virtually), spend time meditating or contemplating the energy of the place. Tune in to the environment, and open yourself to any insights or intuitive feelings that arise.

Engage with Sacred Geometry and Ancient Architecture

- **Action Step**: Study the principles of sacred geometry, as it was a core aspect of ancient civilizations, especially in their architecture and spiritual practices. Learn about the Flower of Life, the Golden Ratio, and how they manifest in the natural world and in ancient structures.

- **Application**: Incorporate sacred geometry into your daily life. This could be as simple as placing symbols around your home or workplace, using them in art, or applying these principles in design. Sacred geometry can serve as a reminder of the interconnectedness of all life and the balance that lost civilizations sought to achieve.

Explore Alternative Theories in Archaeology

- **Action Step**: Research alternative theories on ancient history, lost civilizations, and archaeological anomalies. Read books and watch documentaries from independent researchers who challenge the conventional timeline of human history.

- **Application**: Consider how these alternative narratives could reshape our understanding of the past and inspire us to think differently about the present. Share these ideas with others, fostering curiosity and dialogue about the possibilities that exist outside of mainstream history.

Connect with the Earth and Nature

- **Action Step**: Many ancient civilizations, especially Lemuria, had a deep connection with nature. Start a daily practice of connecting with the Earth, whether through gardening, hiking, or simply spending time in nature.

- **Application**: Use these moments to reflect on the harmony that ancient civilizations maintained with the Earth. Consider how you can incorporate that balance into your life reducing your ecological footprint, living more sustainably, or simply cultivating gratitude for the natural world.

Awaken Your Inner Intuition and Connection to the Past

- **Action Step**: Engage in meditative or contemplative practices to awaken your intuition and sense of connection to the ancient past. Visualization exercises can help you tap into collective memories or "Akashic records" that may hold the wisdom of these civilizations.

- **Application**: Begin a meditation practice where you visualize yourself exploring the halls of an ancient library, a temple, or a sacred space from one of these lost civilizations. Allow your subconscious to reveal symbols, messages, or insights that may help you understand the mysteries of the past and how they apply to your own spiritual journey.

Foster a Community of Curiosity and Exploration

- **Action Step**: Engage with others who are interested in the mysteries of human origins. Join online forums, attend lectures or webinars, or start a book club focusing on ancient wisdom and lost civilizations.

- **Application**: Share your discoveries, questions, and reflections with a community of like-minded individuals. Collective curiosity often leads to new insights and breakthroughs. Together, we can deepen our understanding of humanity's origins and its implications for our future.

Bringing Ancient Wisdom Into the Modern World

By exploring the mysterious origins of humanity, you not only uncover the lost knowledge of past civilizations but also reconnect with the deeper, timeless wisdom that has shaped human development across millennia. The ancient world holds a mirror to our present, showing us both the heights of human achievement and the dangers of losing touch with our spiritual, ecological, and creative potential. By taking practical steps to study, integrate, and apply this ancient wisdom, you can bring a sense of purpose, connection, and innovation into your own life.

Ultimately, the mysteries of our past are not just history, they are living, breathing elements of the human story, waiting for us to rediscover, honor, and build upon as we navigate the future.

A Shaman's Insights on Ancient Wisdom and Lost Civilizations

Maria Lunas, a contemporary shaman and spiritual healer, offers her perspective on the connection between lost civilizations like Lemuria and modern spiritual practices:

"In my practice as a shaman, I often guide people to reconnect with their ancestors, the earth, and the wisdom that flows through all living things. But there's another layer a deeper layer that I've always sensed: the presence of an ancient wisdom that predates our current understanding of history.

"Through meditation, rituals, and vision journeys, I've come to believe that we are the descendants of civilizations that were deeply in tune with the energies of the earth and the cosmos. Lemuria, as I understand it, was one such civilization. They lived in harmony with the earth, their consciousness expanded beyond the physical realm, and their understanding of spirituality went far beyond what we practice today. I've encountered spirit guides who have shown me glimpses of these times, where human beings were not just surviving, but thriving in ways that we can barely comprehend now."

"For those who are open to the ancient wisdom that lies dormant within our DNA, we can reawaken these abilities. We're not just descendants of these lost civilizations we are their continuation, and their wisdom still flows through us. It's our duty to listen, to remember, and to bring that knowledge back into the world."

An Amateur Historian's Discovery of Göbekli Tepe

Liam O'Connell, an amateur historian and travel enthusiast, recounts his experience visiting Göbekli Tepe, one of the oldest archaeological sites ever discovered:

"When I first heard about Göbekli Tepe, I couldn't believe it. A site that predates Stonehenge and the Pyramids, built with an understanding of architecture and spirituality that seemed out of

place for the time. I had to see it for myself. Standing among the towering stone pillars, I felt a deep connection to something ancient and mysterious. Who were these people who built this site over 12,000 years ago? And why did they build it with such precision and care?"

"The intricate carvings on the stones the animals, the symbols they all felt like messages from a distant time, trying to tell us something about their world. As I stood there, I began to wonder: what if the history we've been taught is only the tip of the iceberg? What if civilizations like this existed, thrived, and then disappeared, leaving behind only whispers of their existence?"

"Göbekli Tepe challenged my understanding of human history, and I left with more questions than answers. But I also felt a sense of awe of being connected to something far larger than myself. The past isn't dead; it's alive in these stones, in these symbols, and in the mysteries that we're only just beginning to uncover."

PART II: SHADOWS AND ILLUMINATIONS

CHAPTER 4:
SUPPRESSED
TECHNOLOGIES AND
HIDDEN ADVANCES
REVEALING THE
SECRETS KEPT
FROM HUMANITY

"In every generation, there are breakthroughs so profound that they threaten to reshape the world. But sometimes, those breakthroughs are buried not by time, but by those who fear their power."
Dr. Evelyn Carter

Prologue

Throughout history, there have been whispers of incredible

technologies and revolutionary ideas that could have changed the course of human civilization had they not been suppressed. From energy sources that defy conventional understanding to medical advances that could cure seemingly incurable diseases, these hidden technologies have often been kept from the public eye by powerful interests seeking to maintain control. As Dr. Evelyn Carter sits among stacks of declassified documents, faded patents, and confidential testimonies, she begins to piece together a tapestry of innovation, suppression, and untapped potential. This chapter delves into some of the most controversial suppressed technologies, examining how they could have transformed society and exploring the forces that conspired to keep them hidden.

The Innovations of Nikola Tesla and Other Forgotten Geniuses

Few figures exemplify the brilliance and tragedy of suppressed technology more than Nikola Tesla. His groundbreaking inventions promised to revolutionize energy, communication, and even the way we understand reality itself. Yet, much of his work was stifled by financial barriers, corporate sabotage, and mysterious disappearances of key patents.

Tesla's Dream of Free Energy

- **Wardenclyffe Tower: Wireless Power Transmission**
  Tesla's most ambitious project, the Wardenclyffe Tower, was designed to transmit electricity wirelessly across vast distances, tapping into the Earth's natural electromagnetic field. This technology, which Tesla called "World Wireless System," aimed to provide free and unlimited energy to everyone, bypassing traditional power lines.

- **Obstacles Encountered**
  The project's main backer, J.P. Morgan, famously

withdrew funding after realizing that Tesla's technology could not be metered and monetized in the same way as traditional energy sources. Without financial support, the Wardenclyffe Tower was never completed, and Tesla's dream of free energy was left unrealized.

- **The FBI Files**
Upon Tesla's death in 1943, the U.S. government seized many of his documents and inventions. Some of these papers have never been fully released, leading to speculation that Tesla's discoveries included classified technologies with military or energy implications. Despite multiple Freedom of Information Act requests, many details about Tesla's work remain shrouded in secrecy.

Classified Patents and Secret Projects

- **Project Rainbow and the Philadelphia Experiment**
During World War II, rumors circulated of secret U.S. Navy projects allegedly involving the manipulation of electromagnetic fields to achieve invisibility and teleportation. Known as the Philadelphia Experiment, these accounts suggest that Tesla's work on electromagnetic fields was adapted for military use, with catastrophic results. Although officially denied, numerous eyewitness accounts and declassified documents hint at a covert attempt to harness technologies that could bend the laws of physics.

- **The Death Ray and Directed Energy Weapons**
Tesla claimed to have developed a weapon capable of destroying aircraft and armies with concentrated beams of energy. Dubbed the "Death Ray," this technology was never fully realized in Tesla's lifetime, but concepts resembling his descriptions have since emerged in military research into directed energy weapons. Some theorists believe that Tesla's original plans were co-opted

and remain hidden in classified defense projects.

- **John Hutchison's Anti-Gravity Experiments**
Canadian inventor John Hutchison claimed to have replicated Tesla's experiments with high-voltage electricity and electromagnetism, resulting in the Hutchison Effect a series of phenomena including levitation, metal distortion, and spontaneous combustion of materials. Despite recorded demonstrations, Hutchison's work has been largely dismissed by mainstream science, and his laboratory was raided multiple times by authorities, adding to the narrative of suppression.

Implications for Modern Society

- **A World Transformed by Free Energy**
If Tesla's vision of wireless, free energy had been realized, the implications for modern society would be profound. The global economy, which is heavily dependent on fossil fuels, could have shifted to a sustainable, decentralized energy model, reducing environmental degradation and geopolitical tensions over energy resources.

- **Disrupting Power Structures**
Technologies that promise free and abundant resources pose a direct threat to established power structures, including energy companies, governments, and financial institutions that rely on scarcity to maintain control. This potential disruption may explain why some of the most revolutionary technologies have been marginalized or actively suppressed.

- **Reviving Forgotten Inventions**
Today, researchers and independent inventors continue to explore Tesla's theories, aiming to recreate his experiments and bring his vision to life. Open-source initiatives and technological crowdfunding have provided

new platforms for these once-forgotten inventions, sparking renewed interest in what was once dismissed as impossible.

Medical Advances and Miraculous Cures

While the technological innovations of the past century have led to remarkable medical advancements, there remains a shadow of unexplored or suppressed treatments that defy conventional medical wisdom. From natural remedies to unexplained healings, the pursuit of alternative medicine has often clashed with mainstream healthcare systems driven by profit and regulation.

Suppressed Natural Remedies

- **Cannabis and Psychedelic Medicines**
  For decades, natural substances like cannabis, psilocybin mushrooms, and ayahuasca have been classified as dangerous drugs, despite mounting evidence of their therapeutic potential. Research shows that these substances can treat a range of conditions, including chronic pain, depression, PTSD, and addiction. However, regulatory and financial barriers have delayed their acceptance and widespread use, often due to the interests of pharmaceutical companies that profit from synthetic alternatives.

- **Laetrile and Vitamin B17**
  Laetrile, derived from apricot seeds and containing Vitamin B17, was once touted as a natural cancer treatment. Despite testimonials from patients who claimed miraculous recoveries, the substance was banned in the United States due to claims of toxicity and lack of scientific evidence. Critics argue that

this suppression was motivated by the pharmaceutical industry's reluctance to embrace natural, non-patentable treatments.

- **Stem Cell Therapy and Regenerative Medicine**
Stem cell therapy has the potential to revolutionize medicine, offering cures for conditions once thought untreatable, such as spinal cord injuries, neurodegenerative diseases, and organ failure. Yet, regulatory restrictions, high costs, and ethical debates have stifled the full exploration of this field. Promising treatments are often available only in a few countries, limiting access to life-saving therapies.

The Role of Big Pharmaceutical Companies

- **Profit vs. Healing**
The pharmaceutical industry, driven by profits, has a vested interest in promoting treatments that generate ongoing revenue, such as daily medications for chronic conditions. Cures, by contrast, threaten the economic model of repeat business. This dynamic has led to allegations that promising cures are suppressed in favor of more lucrative treatments.

- **Ghostwriting and Data Manipulation**
Pharmaceutical companies have been accused of manipulating clinical trial data, ghostwriting medical research, and aggressively marketing drugs while downplaying side effects. High-profile scandals involving painkillers, antidepressants, and other medications highlight the darker side of an industry that often prioritizes profit over patient well-being.

- **Patents and Access**
The patent system, designed to protect innovation, can also stifle it. By controlling access to essential medicines and technologies, companies can set high prices that

limit availability, particularly in developing countries. This monopoly over life-saving treatments exacerbates global health inequities and restricts the dissemination of potentially revolutionary medical advances.

Cases of Unexplained Healings

- **Spontaneous Remission of Cancer**
  Documented cases exist where patients have experienced spontaneous remission of cancer without conventional treatment. While such occurrences are rare and not fully understood, they suggest that the human body has untapped healing potential that could be harnessed with a better understanding of immunology, genetics, and environmental factors.

- **Faith Healing and the Placebo Effect**
  From miraculous recoveries attributed to prayer and faith healers to the measurable impact of the placebo effect, these cases highlight the complex relationship between mind, body, and belief. While often dismissed by mainstream medicine, these phenomena suggest that psychological and spiritual factors can significantly influence physical health, challenging the materialist view of healing.

- **Energy Healing and Alternative Therapies**
  Modalities such as Reiki, acupuncture, and other forms of energy healing are often relegated to the fringe of medical practice, yet they have demonstrated measurable benefits in numerous studies. As science continues to explore the impact of bioelectric fields on cellular function, these ancient practices may one day be recognized as legitimate components of an integrated medical approach.

Implications for Modern Healthcare

Embracing Integrative Medicine

- **A Holistic Approach**: The integration of suppressed and alternative therapies with conventional medicine could revolutionize healthcare, offering more comprehensive and personalized treatment options. Embracing a holistic approach that includes nutrition, mental health, energy work, and traditional medicine could lead to better patient outcomes and a deeper understanding of human health.

- **Reducing Dependence on Pharmaceuticals**: Widespread acceptance of natural remedies and alternative therapies could reduce the global reliance on pharmaceuticals, decreasing side effects, lowering healthcare costs, and promoting wellness over symptom management.

Ethical Challenges and the Future of Medicine

- **Regulation vs. Innovation**: Balancing the need for rigorous testing and regulation with the need to innovate poses a significant challenge. Breaking down the barriers that prevent promising treatments from reaching patients will require rethinking the regulatory landscape to prioritize healing over profit.

- **Empowering Patients**: As access to information grows, patients are becoming more empowered to explore alternative treatments and make informed decisions about their healthcare. This shift challenges the traditional power dynamics of the medical field and encourages a more collaborative approach to health.

The Potential of Rediscovered Knowledge

- **Reviving Lost Cures**: Rediscovering suppressed or forgotten medical treatments could open new avenues for healing. From ancient herbal remedies to energy-based therapies, the vast repository of historical medical knowledge remains an untapped resource that could complement modern medicine.

- **The Intersection of Science and Spirituality**: As our understanding of the mind-body connection deepens, there is growing recognition that healing is not just a physical process but a holistic one that encompasses the mental, emotional, and spiritual dimensions of the human experience.

Conclusion

The suppression of transformative technologies and medical advances is a reminder of the power dynamics that shape our world. Whether through financial interests, regulatory hurdles, or the complexities of human nature, the hidden innovations of the past continue to whisper to us from the shadows. By uncovering and embracing these lost or suppressed technologies, we have the opportunity to not only rewrite our history but also redefine our future. It is a journey of rediscovery, one that challenges us to look beyond what is known and venture into the uncharted territory of human potential.

"Suppressed technologies are not lost forever; they are

waiting to be rediscovered by those brave enough to see beyond the barriers of fear and control."

Dr. Evelyn Carter

Reflection Questions:

How have financial and political interests historically influenced the suppression of transformative technologies and medical advancements? What impact has this had on modern society?

What are the ethical implications of suppressing technologies that could benefit humanity, and how can we ensure that future innovations are shared rather than hidden?

How can modern society embrace and integrate suppressed or alternative technologies in ways that challenge existing power structures and improve global well-being?

CHAPTER 5: THE INNOVATIONS OF NIKOLA TESLA AND OTHER FORGOTTEN GENIUSES EXPLORING THE HIDDEN TECHNOLOGIES THAT COULD HAVE CHANGED THE WORLD

"The future belongs to those who dare to explore the limits of possibility. For Tesla and others like him, those limits were boundless if only the world had listened."
Dr. Armand Wallace

Prologue

Nikola Tesla is often remembered as the brilliant but tragic inventor whose visionary ideas were ahead of his time. But Tesla was not alone; he was part of a broader movement of forgotten geniuses scientists, inventors, and thinkers whose groundbreaking work promised to reshape humanity's future. From free energy to antigravity, their innovations could have altered the course of history, but instead, many were buried, suppressed, or left unrecognized. As Dr. Armand Wallace digs through the archives of lost patents, obscure writings, and the remnants of secretive experiments, he discovers a narrative of missed opportunities and hidden potential. This chapter uncovers the untold stories of Tesla and other forgotten minds, delving into the technologies that were on the verge of changing the world, and the powerful forces that sought to keep them hidden.

Free Energy and Energy Discoveries

One of Tesla's most revolutionary ideas was the concept of free energy harnessing the abundant and untapped forces of nature to provide unlimited, clean power to everyone on the planet. His work in this field, though often marginalized, laid the groundwork for what could have been a new era of energy independence.

Tesla's Vision of a Wireless World

- **The Wardenclyffe Tower**: Tesla's most ambitious project, the Wardenclyffe Tower, was designed not only as a global communication hub but also as a means to transmit wireless electricity. Tesla envisioned a world where energy could be freely transmitted through the

Earth's atmosphere, making power accessible to even the most remote corners of the globe.

- **The Technology Behind the Tower**: The tower's design was based on Tesla's understanding of resonant energy. Using his Tesla Coil a high-frequency oscillator capable of producing high-voltage currents Tesla planned to tap into the ionosphere, a natural layer of charged particles surrounding the Earth, to create a limitless energy network. This system would have allowed power to be broadcast without wires, eliminating the need for power plants and electrical grids as we know them.

- **Sabotage and Abandonment**: Despite his genius, Tesla's vision was thwarted by financial challenges and powerful industrial interests. J.P. Morgan, initially a key investor, withdrew support when he realized that wireless energy could not be monetized in the traditional sense. Left without funding, Tesla's dream of a wireless world was abandoned, and the tower was eventually dismantled.

The Earth's Natural Resonance: Schumann Waves

- **Harnessing the Earth's Energy**: Tesla believed that the Earth itself was a giant conductor of energy. His experiments with the Earth's natural frequency, later known as Schumann Resonance, suggested that energy could be harnessed from the ground and air. This concept aligns with modern theories of electromagnetic energy harvesting, which seek to convert natural frequencies into usable power.

- **Implications for Modern Energy**: If fully realized, Tesla's theories could have paved the way for sustainable, decentralized energy solutions that would revolutionize the way we power our homes, industries, and technologies. Modern researchers are still exploring ways to harness these natural energy sources, inspired by Tesla's pioneering work.

Zero-Point Energy and the Search for Unlimited Power

- **Beyond Tesla**: Zero-point energy is the theoretical concept that even in a vacuum devoid of matter, there exists a residual energy that permeates all of space. This energy, sometimes referred to as the "quantum vacuum," holds the potential for virtually limitless power.

- **The Casimir Effect**: Discovered in the mid-20th century, the Casimir Effect provides experimental evidence of zero-point energy. This phenomenon occurs when two metal plates placed very close together experience a measurable force due to changes in the quantum vacuum. The Casimir Effect has led some physicists to speculate that zero-point energy could one day be harnessed as a power source, echoing Tesla's early ideas.

- **The Implications of Zero-Point Energy**: If this energy could be tapped, it would provide a nearly infinite supply of power with no environmental impact, ending reliance on fossil fuels and transforming global energy systems. However, technological barriers and skepticism from mainstream science continue to keep zero-point energy in the realm of speculative research.

Classified Patents and Secret Projects

Many of Tesla's patents and those of other inventors have remained classified or inaccessible to the public, fueling speculation about the existence of suppressed technologies that could revolutionize energy, transportation, and even warfare.

Tesla's Death Ray: The Peace Ray

- **Directed Energy Weapons**: Tesla claimed to have invented a weapon that could shoot concentrated beams of energy capable of destroying aircraft, tanks, and any other targets from great distances. He described it as a defensive weapon, intended to create an "invisible wall of energy" that could protect nations without the need for conventional arms.

- **Government Interest and Secrecy**: Although Tesla offered his invention to various governments, including the U.S., there was little public acknowledgment of any official development. After Tesla's death, the U.S. government seized his papers, many of which were never declassified, leading to speculation that his concepts were adapted into secret military projects.

- **Modern Directed Energy Weapons**: Today, directed energy weapons are a reality, with military research into laser systems, microwave weapons, and other energy-based technologies. Whether these modern developments are based on Tesla's original designs remains an open question, but the similarities suggest a continuation of his pioneering ideas.

The X-Ray Gun and Particle Beams

- **Early Innovations in Radiation**: Tesla was also a pioneer in the field of radiation technology, developing early forms of X-ray imaging long before their widespread use in medicine. He envisioned using particle beams for both medical and industrial applications, but his work was cut short due to lack of funding and the dangerous nature of early radiation experiments.

- **Potential Applications**: If fully developed, Tesla's X-ray and particle beam technologies could have advanced fields such as medical diagnostics, material science, and even energy generation. However, concerns about safety and the impact of radiation limited their early exploration.

Other Forgotten Geniuses: Thomas Townsend Brown and Antigravity

- **Electrogravitics and Antigravity**: Thomas Townsend Brown, an American physicist, explored the relationship between electromagnetism and gravity, proposing that high-voltage electrical fields could counteract gravitational forces. His work on "electrogravitics" suggested the possibility of antigravity propulsion, which could revolutionize transportation by enabling frictionless, silent flight.

- **Military Interest and Classified Research**: Brown's research caught the attention of military contractors and the U.S. government, leading to classified projects that explored antigravity and advanced propulsion systems. Although these technologies were never publicly developed, the secrecy surrounding Brown's work has fueled rumors that antigravity technologies exist within classified military programs.

- **The Implications of Antigravity**: If antigravity technologies were fully realized, they would revolutionize air and space travel, enabling faster, more efficient transportation without the constraints of current propulsion systems. The potential applications extend to everything from civilian transportation to space exploration, making the suppression of these technologies a significant loss for humanity.

Implications for Modern Society

The existence of suppressed or forgotten technologies raises profound ethical and practical questions about the control of knowledge, the monopolization of innovation, and the future of technological development.

Transforming Energy and Industry

- **A New Energy Paradigm**: The realization of Tesla's free energy technologies would disrupt the global energy industry, eliminating the need for oil, coal, and even nuclear power. This shift could reduce environmental degradation, lower energy costs, and democratize access to power, especially in developing regions.

- **Decentralized Power**: Free energy would enable decentralized power generation, reducing the influence of centralized energy companies and empowering individuals and communities to manage their own energy needs. This shift could also mitigate conflicts over energy resources, fostering global stability.

Breaking the Barriers of Transportation

- **Antigravity and Beyond**: The development of antigravity and advanced propulsion technologies could lead to revolutionary changes in transportation, making air travel faster, quieter, and more sustainable. The implications for space exploration are equally significant, potentially enabling long-distance space travel and colonization efforts far beyond current capabilities.

- **The End of Conventional Vehicles**: With antigravity, the need for traditional vehicles with engines, wheels, and roads could be eliminated, leading to new urban designs and transportation systems that prioritize efficiency and environmental harmony.

Reclaiming Suppressed Knowledge

- **The Role of Open Science**: To unlock the potential of suppressed technologies, it is essential to promote open science, where research is transparent, collaborative, and accessible. By breaking down barriers to innovation, we can ensure that future technological advancements are shared for the benefit of all humanity.

- **Challenges of Regulation and Safety**: Bringing suppressed technologies to light will require careful consideration of safety, regulation, and ethical implications. Balancing innovation with public safety and addressing potential misuse of powerful technologies is crucial for responsible development.

Conclusion

The innovations of Tesla and other forgotten geniuses represent a lost chapter in the story of human progress one filled with promise, potential, and profound implications for our future. The suppression of these technologies serves as a cautionary tale about the dangers of monopolizing knowledge and the importance of keeping the pursuit of discovery open to all. By rediscovering and embracing these hidden advances, we have the opportunity to reshape our world, realizing the dreams of those who dared to look beyond the boundaries of their time.

"The forgotten geniuses of history are not truly lost; their

ideas remain, waiting to be rediscovered by those who believe that the impossible is just the beginning."
Dr. Armand Wallace

Reflection Questions:

How would the widespread adoption of suppressed technologies like free energy or antigravity propulsion transform modern society? What are the potential benefits and challenges of such a shift?

Why do you think certain technologies have been suppressed or forgotten throughout history? How can we prevent this from happening with future innovations?

What lessons can we learn from the stories of Nikola Tesla and other forgotten geniuses about the importance of open innovation, collaboration, and the responsible use of technology?

CHAPTER 6: MEDICAL ADVANCES AND MIRACULOUS CURES UNVEILING THE HIDDEN POTENTIAL OF NATURAL REMEDIES AND ALTERNATIVE THERAPIES

"The greatest secrets in medicine are not hidden in distant labs or guarded by pharmaceutical patents they are often right in front of us, waiting to be rediscovered."
  Dr. Sylvia Manning

Prologue

For centuries, humanity has sought cures for disease and

ways to extend life, from ancient herbal remedies to cutting-edge genetic therapies. Yet, not all medical advances are celebrated or made accessible to the public. Often, the most groundbreaking treatments are obscured by regulatory barriers, financial interests, and institutional resistance to change. In the quiet sanctuary of a holistic healing clinic, Dr. Sylvia Manning studies the long-forgotten texts of ancient medicine, testimonies of unexplained healings, and suppressed clinical trials. Her mission is to uncover the hidden potential of natural remedies and alternative therapies that could transform healthcare as we know it. This chapter explores the world of suppressed medical advances, delving into the financial and political forces that keep these cures in the shadows and the miraculous recoveries that defy conventional explanations.

Suppressed Natural Remedies

Throughout history, plants and natural substances have been used to treat a wide range of ailments. Yet, as modern medicine advanced, many of these ancient remedies were pushed aside in favor of synthetic drugs, often driven by the profit motives of pharmaceutical companies. Some of these natural treatments, however, hold untapped potential for curing diseases that remain a challenge to modern medicine.

The Healing Power of Medicinal Plants

- **Cannabis and Cannabinoids**: Once vilified and banned globally, cannabis is now emerging as a potent therapeutic agent. Cannabinoids, the active compounds found in cannabis, have been shown to effectively treat chronic pain, epilepsy, anxiety, and even cancer. Despite a growing body of evidence, regulatory hurdles and the influence of pharmaceutical companies have slowed the adoption of cannabis-based therapies in many regions.

- **Psychedelics**: **Psilocybin, LSD, and**

Ayahuasca: Psychedelic substances, traditionally used in indigenous rituals, are now being studied for their profound impact on mental health. Psilocybin (magic mushrooms), LSD, and ayahuasca have shown promise in treating depression, PTSD, addiction, and anxiety, often succeeding where conventional medications fail. Despite their potential, these substances remain heavily regulated due to their historical stigma and legal classification as dangerous drugs.

- **Turmeric and Curcumin**: Known as a powerful anti-inflammatory agent, turmeric has been used in traditional medicine for millennia. Its active compound, curcumin, has demonstrated anti-cancer, anti-viral, and antioxidant properties. Despite extensive research supporting its benefits, turmeric's therapeutic potential is often overshadowed by synthetic alternatives, many of which come with a higher price tag and more side effects.

Banned or Restricted Natural Treatments

- **Laetrile (Vitamin B17)**: Derived from apricot kernels, Laetrile (also known as amygdalin or Vitamin B17) was once considered a promising cancer treatment. Despite anecdotal reports of tumor shrinkage and patient recoveries, the U.S. FDA banned Laetrile in the 1970s, citing a lack of scientific evidence and potential toxicity. Critics argue that its suppression was driven more by the interests of pharmaceutical companies than by safety concerns, and underground markets for Laetrile persist to this day.

- **Essiac Tea**: A blend of herbs originally used by indigenous Canadian tribes, Essiac tea became famous in the 1920s when nurse Rene Caisse began using it to treat cancer patients. Despite testimonials of miraculous recoveries, the tea's effectiveness has never been formally acknowledged by mainstream medicine, and regulatory bodies have restricted its use, often citing insufficient clinical evidence.

- **Kambo: Frog Venom Therapy**: Used traditionally in Amazonian tribes, Kambo involves applying the venom of the Giant Monkey Frog to the skin, inducing a powerful purgative and immune-boosting effect. Practitioners claim that Kambo can detoxify the body, improve mental clarity, and even treat chronic illness. However, due to its intense effects and lack of formal studies, Kambo remains controversial and is often labeled as dangerous by medical authorities.

Modern Rediscoveries and Integration of Natural Therapies

- **The Revival of Herbal Medicine**: In recent years, there has been a resurgence of interest in herbal medicine, spurred by the desire for natural, low-cost alternatives to pharmaceuticals. Integrative health practices that combine conventional and alternative therapies are gaining traction, with patients increasingly seeking herbal treatments, acupuncture, and nutritional guidance as part of their overall health strategy.

- **The Role of Functional Medicine**: Functional medicine, a holistic approach that focuses on treating the root causes of illness rather than symptoms, has begun to incorporate many suppressed natural remedies. This approach emphasizes personalized care, diet, lifestyle changes, and the use of supplements, herbs, and other natural treatments to promote healing.

- **Regulation and the Fight for Legitimacy**: Despite the growing popularity of natural remedies, regulatory frameworks often lag behind, making it difficult for patients to access these treatments. Advocates for natural medicine continue to push for clinical trials, better regulation, and the removal of restrictions that prevent these therapies from reaching those in need.

The Role of Big Pharmaceutical Companies

The pharmaceutical industry, while responsible for some of the greatest medical advances of the modern era, is also driven by profit motives that can conflict with the broader public interest. Patents, competition, and the high cost of drug development often lead companies to prioritize profit over patient welfare, resulting in the suppression or sidelining of cheaper, natural, or unpatentable treatments.

The Profit Motive and the Suppression of Cures

- **Chronic Treatments vs. Cures**: Pharmaceutical companies often profit more from chronic treatments that require lifelong adherence than from one-time cures. This financial incentive can lead to a focus on developing drugs that manage symptoms rather than those that could eradicate diseases altogether. Critics argue that this model leaves patients dependent on expensive medications rather than exploring potentially more effective, natural, or holistic cures.

- **Patent Monopolies and Market Control**: Patents grant exclusive rights to drug manufacturers, allowing them to set high prices without competition. This system, while designed to encourage innovation, can also stifle it. Companies may avoid developing or releasing drugs that cannot be patented or that threaten their existing market share, even if those drugs are more effective or safer for patients.

- **Conflicts of Interest and Influence on Research**: Pharmaceutical companies often fund clinical trials, which can lead to conflicts of interest in the design, execution, and reporting of results. Ghostwriting, selective publication, and the suppression of negative findings are all tactics used to present drugs in the most favorable light, sometimes at the expense of patient safety.

High-Profile Cases of Suppression and Scandal

- **The Vioxx Scandal**: Vioxx, a painkiller manufactured by Merck, was once widely prescribed before it was found to significantly increase the risk of heart attack and stroke. Internal documents later revealed that Merck had suppressed data about these risks, leading to a massive recall and a public outcry over the company's handling of the drug.

- **The Opioid Crisis**: Pharmaceutical companies like Purdue Pharma aggressively marketed opioid painkillers, downplaying their addictive potential. The resulting opioid epidemic has caused widespread addiction, overdoses, and deaths, highlighting the devastating consequences of prioritizing profit over public health.

- **Tamiflu and the Flu Treatment Controversy**: During the swine flu pandemic, governments worldwide stockpiled Tamiflu, an antiviral drug produced by Roche. However, subsequent investigations revealed that much of the clinical data on Tamiflu's efficacy was hidden, and the drug's benefits were less significant than advertised. The case underscored the dangers of withholding data and the influence of pharmaceutical lobbying on public health policy.

Financial and Regulatory Barriers to Alternative Therapies

- **High Costs of Clinical Trials**: The cost of bringing a new drug to market can exceed a billion dollars, making it nearly impossible for smaller companies, universities, or independent researchers to develop and test alternative treatments. This financial barrier favors large pharmaceutical companies with the resources to navigate regulatory hurdles and market dominance.

- **Regulatory Restrictions on Natural Remedies**: Natural substances, unlike patented drugs, cannot be easily monetized or exclusively owned, leading to less financial incentive for companies to invest in their development. Regulatory bodies often impose strict guidelines on natural remedies, requiring evidence from costly clinical trials that few can afford, effectively suppressing access to potentially life-saving therapies.

- **Public Mistrust and the Rise of DIY Medicine**: Growing public awareness of pharmaceutical malpractices has led many to seek alternative treatments outside of conventional medicine. This trend, while empowering, also carries risks, as patients may turn to unproven or unsafe remedies without proper guidance. The challenge lies in balancing the regulation of alternative therapies with ensuring access to effective, safe treatments.

Cases of Unexplained Healings

While many medical miracles are dismissed as anecdotal or unscientific, there is a growing body of evidence supporting the idea that unexplained healings are not only possible but may hold the key to understanding the full potential of the human body's capacity to heal.

Spontaneous Remission and Unexplained Recoveries

- **Cancer Remission**: Spontaneous remission of cancer, though rare, is a documented phenomenon where patients recover without conventional treatment. Cases of tumors shrinking or disappearing entirely defy current medical understanding and suggest that the body may have innate mechanisms to combat disease under certain conditions.

- **Near-Death Experiences and Healing**: Some patients report experiencing profound spiritual or near-death experiences that coincide with unexpected healing. These accounts often include feelings of intense peace, visions of light or divine beings, and a renewed sense of purpose, followed by remarkable physical recoveries.

- **Placebo Effect**: The placebo effect demonstrates the powerful impact of belief on health outcomes. In clinical trials, patients receiving inert treatments often show significant improvements simply because they believe they are receiving real medicine. This effect highlights the mind's capacity to influence the body's healing processes, challenging conventional notions of medical intervention.

Energy Healing and Ancient Practices

- **Reiki and Biofield Therapies**: Energy healing modalities like Reiki focus on the transfer of healing energy through the practitioner's hands, channeling what is believed to be universal life force energy into the patient. While scientific evidence remains limited, many patients report relief from pain, stress, and illness, suggesting that the energetic component of healing deserves further exploration.

- **Acupuncture and Traditional Chinese Medicine**: Rooted in thousands of years of practice, acupuncture and other traditional Chinese medicine approaches are based on the manipulation of the body's energy flow, or "qi." These treatments are increasingly recognized by Western medicine for their efficacy in managing pain, reducing stress, and promoting overall wellness.

- **Shamanic Healing and Plant Medicine**: Indigenous healing practices, including shamanism and the use of sacred plants, offer a holistic approach that addresses the spiritual, mental, and physical aspects of illness. Ayahuasca, peyote, and other psychoactive plants are used in ceremonial contexts to promote healing and self-awareness, often leading to profound psychological and emotional breakthroughs.

Integrating Spiritual and Scientific Approaches

- **The Rise of Integrative Medicine**: The growing acceptance of integrative medicine, which combines conventional treatments with alternative approaches, reflects a broader cultural shift toward a more holistic understanding of health. By acknowledging the role of the mind, spirit, and community in healing, integrative medicine offers a more comprehensive approach to patient care.

- **Future Research into Unexplained Healings**: While many unexplained healings remain poorly understood, advancing research in fields like psychoneuroimmunology, the study of how the mind affects the immune system, offers hope for unlocking the secrets of spontaneous recovery. Recognizing the interconnectedness of body, mind, and spirit could revolutionize how we approach health and disease.

Implications for Modern Healthcare

Rethinking the Role of Medicine

- **Beyond the Biomedical Model**: The dominance of the biomedical model, which views disease purely in terms of physical processes, is increasingly being challenged by approaches that consider the psychological, social, and spiritual dimensions of health. Embracing a broader view of medicine could lead to more effective treatments and a deeper understanding of the human experience.

- **Patient-Centered Care**: Shifting toward patient-centered care that values the individual's beliefs, experiences, and preferences can improve health outcomes and foster a more compassionate healthcare system. This approach encourages collaboration between doctors, patients, and alternative practitioners to create personalized treatment plans.

Expanding Access to Alternative Therapies

- **Lowering Regulatory Barriers**: Reforming regulatory frameworks to allow for the safe integration of alternative therapies could expand access to treatments that are currently restricted. Supporting clinical research into natural remedies, energy healing, and other alternative approaches would provide the evidence needed to validate their effectiveness.

- **Education and Awareness**: Educating healthcare providers and the public about the benefits and risks of alternative therapies is crucial for informed decision-making. As patients become more involved in their own care, the demand for trustworthy information about complementary treatments will continue to grow.

The Potential for a New Healing Paradigm

- **Reclaiming Suppressed Knowledge**: Uncovering the suppressed medical knowledge of the past could lead to breakthroughs in treatment options, reducing reliance on costly and side-effect-laden pharmaceuticals. By honoring the wisdom of traditional healing practices, we can create a more inclusive and effective healthcare system.

- **Embracing the Mind-Body Connection**: Recognizing the powerful link between mental, emotional, and physical health can revolutionize medical practice, leading to new therapies that harness the body's natural healing abilities. Future research into unexplained healings, energy medicine, and spiritual practices holds the potential to unlock a new era of human health.

Conclusion

The world of suppressed medical advances is a complex landscape of untapped potential, political barriers, and remarkable stories of healing that challenge conventional wisdom. By exploring these hidden corners of medicine, we can rediscover the profound capabilities of the human body, mind, and spirit. As science continues to evolve, the integration of natural remedies, alternative therapies, and holistic approaches could pave the way for a new era of healthcare one that honors the ancient while embracing the future.

"In the end, the most powerful medicine is often not the one that comes from a laboratory, but the one that reconnects us to ourselves, our bodies, and the natural world."
Dr. Sylvia Manning

Reflection Questions:

What are the key factors that have contributed to the suppression of natural remedies and alternative therapies throughout history? How can society work to bring these treatments into the mainstream?

How might the integration of alternative and conventional medicine change the landscape of healthcare? What are the potential benefits and challenges of this approach?

Why do you think unexplained healings occur, and what can these cases teach us about the potential of the human body and mind? How should modern medicine approach these phenomena?

PERSONAL REFLECTIONS AND TESTIMONIES

A Whistleblower's Journey: Unveiling the Shadows

By Daniel Thompson

As a former intelligence analyst for a major government agency, my career was built on secrets. I was entrusted with classified information, briefed on covert operations, and became intimately familiar with the intricate webs woven by shadow governments. For years, I believed that my work was serving the greater good, protecting my country from unseen threats. But over time, the line between defense and deception began to blur.

It started subtly a redacted report here, an unexplained operation there. I began to notice patterns: missions that seemed less about national security and more about advancing certain corporate interests or political agendas. One operation in particular stands out in my memory: a covert action aimed at destabilizing a small, resource-rich nation under the guise of promoting democracy. In reality, it was orchestrated to gain control over valuable mineral deposits essential for high-tech industries.

The tipping point for me came when I was tasked with analyzing surveillance data collected on domestic soil without warrants or oversight. Innocent citizens were being monitored, their privacy violated, all in the name of security. The ethical implications weighed heavily on me. I struggled with the knowledge that our actions were undermining the very freedoms we were sworn to protect.

Haunted by these revelations, I made the difficult decision to become a whistleblower. I gathered evidence of the clandestine operations and unauthorized surveillance programs. The process was fraught with fear and uncertainty. I knew the risks career destruction, legal repercussions, personal safety threats but my conscience left me no choice.

When I leaked the information to investigative journalists, the fallout was immediate. The agency launched an internal witch hunt to identify the source of the leak. Colleagues I once trusted turned their backs on me. Legal battles ensued, and I found myself vilified in the media as a traitor. Yet, despite the personal cost, I felt a profound sense of liberation. The truth was out, and the public began to question the unchecked power wielded by those operating in the shadows.

The exposure led to congressional hearings, policy reforms, and a broader debate about privacy, ethics, and the role of government. While the journey was harrowing, it reaffirmed my belief in the power of truth and the importance of transparency. Today, I advocate for whistleblower protections and work with organizations dedicated to government accountability. My experience taught me that while shadows may conceal, illumination has the power to transform.

The Cost of Truth: A Journalist's Struggle Against Censorship

By Sarah Mitchell

As an investigative journalist, I have always been driven by a relentless pursuit of truth. My career took me to conflict zones, boardrooms, and the corridors of power, where I sought to uncover stories that others preferred to keep hidden. But nothing prepared me for the labyrinthine complexities I encountered when I began investigating the connections between multinational corporations, government agencies, and covert operations.

It started with a tip about a pharmaceutical company conducting unethical drug trials in developing countries. As I dug deeper, I uncovered a network of collusion involving regulatory bodies turning a blind eye, politicians receiving kickbacks, and media outlets suppressing negative coverage due to advertising interests. The more I uncovered, the more dangerous the situation became.

Threatening phone calls became a regular occurrence. Anonymous sources warned me to back off, citing powerful individuals who would stop at nothing to keep their dealings secret. One evening, as I returned home, I found my apartment ransacked. Files were missing, and a chilling message was left scrawled on my wall: "Stay silent."

Determined not to be intimidated, I pressed on. I partnered with international media organizations to ensure that the story would reach a global audience, making it harder for it to be silenced. When the exposé was finally published, it sent shockwaves through the industry. Governments launched investigations, and the public outcry led to policy changes and legal action against those involved.

However, the victory came at a personal cost. I was sued for defamation, my credentials were questioned, and smear campaigns tarnished my reputation. Colleagues distanced themselves, fearing association with a controversial figure. Financially drained and emotionally exhausted, I contemplated giving up journalism altogether.

In the midst of this turmoil, I received a letter from a woman whose child had been a victim of the unethical drug trials. She thanked me for giving a voice to the voiceless and for shedding light on injustices that had been ignored for too long. Her gratitude rekindled my resolve.

I realized that the role of a journalist is not just to report facts but to hold power accountable, to challenge the narratives imposed by those who operate in the shadows. Despite the obstacles, I continue to pursue stories that matter, advocating for press freedom and transparency. The cost of truth is high, but the cost of silence is far greater.

Inside the Corporate Veil: An Insider's Account of Ethical Dilemmas

By Michael Reynolds

For over twenty years, I climbed the corporate ladder at one of the world's leading technology firms. My position granted me access to the inner workings of a company that was shaping the future through innovation. Yet, behind the sleek façade of progress, I witnessed practices that deeply troubled me.

The company was engaged in developing surveillance technologies marketed as tools for national security and law enforcement. Initially, I was proud to be part of creating systems that could prevent crimes and protect citizens. However, I soon discovered that these technologies were being sold to authoritarian regimes known for human rights abuses. The data collected was used not to safeguard the public but to suppress dissent and target minority groups.

Confidential memos revealed that upper management was fully aware of these implications but prioritized profits over ethics. When I raised concerns, I was met with indifference and veiled warnings about jeopardizing my career.

The turning point came when I was asked to lead a project involving the development of facial recognition software with capabilities that infringed on privacy rights. The technology could identify individuals in real-time, track their movements, and compile detailed profiles without their consent. The potential for misuse was enormous.

I faced a moral dilemma: comply and advance, or take a stand and risk everything. I chose the latter. I compiled evidence of the company's practices and submitted an anonymous report to regulatory authorities and human rights organizations.

The aftermath was swift. An internal investigation was launched to identify the whistleblower. I was placed under scrutiny, isolated by colleagues, and eventually pressured into resigning. The public revelations led to a temporary dip in the company's stock prices and a flurry of media attention, but ultimately, minimal action was taken against the corporation.

Disillusioned but undeterred, I joined a non-profit organization dedicated to promoting ethical technology development. I now work with tech companies to implement frameworks that prioritize human rights and privacy. My experience taught me that the pursuit of innovation must be balanced with responsibility, and that individuals within organizations have the power and the duty to advocate for ethical practices.

Unveiling the Enigma: A Former Secret Society Member Speaks Out

By Sophia Martinez

For over a decade, I was a member of an exclusive organization that operated behind the scenes of global finance and politics. The allure was irresistible access to influential networks, the promise of shaping policies, and the sense of being part of an elite group entrusted with guiding humanity's future. I joined with the belief that we were working towards a greater good.

Our meetings were held in opulent, undisclosed locations, where conversations flowed freely under the cloak of confidentiality. The agenda often included discussions on economic strategies, technological advancements, and geopolitical affairs. Initially, it seemed we were genuinely contributing to global progress.

However, as I rose through the ranks, I began to notice

a disturbing undercurrent. Decisions were being made that prioritized power consolidation over public welfare. We manipulated markets, influenced elections, and orchestrated events that caused instability all to serve the interests of a select few. Ethical considerations were dismissed as obstacles to our objectives.

The turning point for me came during a summit where plans were unveiled to exploit a natural disaster in a developing country for financial gain. The cold calculation of human suffering as an opportunity was a line I could not cross. The realization that I was part of a mechanism perpetuating inequality and oppression was devastating.

I faced a harrowing choice: remain complicit or risk everything to expose the truth. Gathering evidence meticulously, I prepared to reveal the organization's machinations. Aware of the dangers surveillance, character assassination, even threats to my safety I proceeded with caution.

I collaborated with international investigative journalists, providing them with documents and recordings that unveiled the depth of the organization's influence. When the exposé was published, it sent shockwaves worldwide. Governments initiated probes, public outcry demanded accountability, and the organization's veil of secrecy began to lift.

Retaliation was swift. I faced legal battles, smear campaigns, and isolation. Yet, the support from activists, ethical leaders, and ordinary citizens reaffirmed my conviction. Today, I advocate for transparency and ethical governance, working to dismantle the structures that allow such shadowy powers to thrive. My journey taught me that true progress is rooted in integrity, and that one voice can indeed make a difference.

Echoes from the Dark Web: A Cybersecurity Expert's Revelation

By Alex Nguyen

As a cybersecurity specialist, my world revolved around code, encryption, and the ceaseless battle against digital threats. Employed by a leading tech firm contracted by various governments, I was part of a team tasked with fortifying defenses against cyber-attacks. The work was challenging but fulfilling until I stumbled upon a secret project that changed everything.

Late one night, while debugging a system, I discovered a hidden backdoor embedded within our software. This backdoor allowed unauthorized access to vast amounts of user data emails, messages, financial transactions without detection. At first, I thought it was a flaw, but further investigation revealed it was intentionally designed.

Disturbed, I approached my supervisor, who dismissed my concerns and warned me to drop the matter. Unsatisfied, I dug deeper and uncovered communications indicating that the backdoor was part of a government surveillance initiative bypassing legal protocols and oversight.

Realizing the implications that millions of people's privacy was being violated under the guise of security I faced a moral dilemma. Remaining silent meant being complicit; speaking out risked my career and possibly my freedom.

I decided to act. Anonymously, I leaked the information to digital rights organizations and journalists specializing in cybersecurity. The story broke, igniting debates over privacy, government overreach, and the ethical responsibilities of tech companies. Public pressure led to congressional hearings, and the backdoor was eventually closed.

The fallout was personal and professional. I was identified, terminated from my position, and faced legal threats. However, the support from privacy advocates and the positive change that resulted reinforced my belief that ethical responsibility outweighs personal risk.

I now work with non-profits dedicated to promoting digital privacy and security. My experience highlights the importance of vigilance in the digital age and the power individuals have to challenge systems that infringe upon fundamental rights.

The Healer's Burden: Exposing the Pharmaceutical Industry

By Dr. Elena Rodriguez

As a medical researcher specializing in epidemiology, my career was devoted to combating diseases and improving public health. Employed by a prominent pharmaceutical company, I was excited to contribute to developing life-saving medications. However, over time, I witnessed practices that deeply conflicted with my ethical beliefs.

During a project involving a new drug intended to treat

a widespread illness, clinical trial data showed significant adverse effects that outweighed the benefits. When I presented these findings, I was pressured to alter the results to favor a positive outcome. The justification was that the drug's profitability was essential for funding future research.

Unwilling to compromise scientific integrity, I refused. In response, I was removed from the project, and my access to data was restricted. Colleagues who sympathized were silenced or reassigned. It became evident that profit was prioritized over patient safety.

Determined to protect potential patients, I compiled the unaltered data and submitted it to regulatory authorities and medical journals. The company's attempts to suppress the information were intense they discredited my professional reputation, initiated legal action, and spread rumors of misconduct.

Despite the onslaught, the truth prevailed. Regulatory bodies launched investigations, the drug's approval was halted, and the company's unethical practices were exposed. My actions sparked a broader discussion about transparency in pharmaceutical research and the need for stricter oversight.

While my career within the industry was effectively ended, I transitioned to academia, focusing on ethical research practices and mentoring the next generation of scientists. I also advocate for policy reforms to ensure that public health interests are not overshadowed by corporate greed. The journey reaffirmed my commitment to the Hippocratic Oath and the belief that integrity in science is non-negotiable.

PRACTICAL APPLICATIONS AND ACTION STEPS

Empowering Individuals to Illuminate the Shadows

The shadows cast by covert operations, shadow governments, and clandestine alliances can seem impenetrable. However, history has shown that collective action and informed citizenship can bring about significant change. Here are practical steps individuals can take to promote transparency, protect democratic values, and hold powerful institutions accountable.

Stay Informed and Educate Others

- **Diversify Information Sources:** Rely on multiple news outlets, including international and independent media, to gain a broader perspective on global events. Be cautious of echo chambers and seek out investigative journalism that delves beneath surface narratives.

- **Fact-Checking:** Use reputable fact-checking organizations to verify information, especially before sharing it on social media. Misinformation can spread quickly and undermine efforts to hold institutions accountable.

- **Educate Yourself on Policies and Legislation:** Understand the laws and regulations that govern surveillance, privacy, and government transparency. Knowledge is a powerful tool in advocating for change.

Support Whistleblowers and Journalists

- **Advocate for Whistleblower Protections:** Support legislation that safeguards whistleblowers from retaliation. Recognize the vital role they play in exposing unethical practices.

- **Subscribe to Independent Media:** Financially support journalists and media outlets that prioritize investigative reporting and operate free from corporate or governmental influence.

- **Engage on Social Media:** Amplify the voices of journalists and whistleblowers by sharing their work responsibly. Online platforms can be powerful tools for raising awareness.

Promote Transparency and Accountability

- **Participate in Local Governance:** Attend town hall meetings, engage with elected officials, and voice concerns about issues related to transparency and ethical governance.

- **Demand Open Data Initiatives:** Encourage governments and institutions to adopt open data policies, making information accessible to the public for scrutiny and analysis.

- **Support Transparency Organizations:** Donate to or volunteer with organizations like Transparency International, the Electronic Frontier Foundation, or the Freedom of the Press Foundation that work towards government accountability and the protection of civil liberties.

Protect Privacy and Advocate for Digital Rights

- **Use Encryption and Privacy Tools:** Protect your personal data by using encrypted messaging apps, VPNs, and secure browsers. Awareness of digital footprints can mitigate unauthorized surveillance.

- **Educate Others on Digital Literacy:** Help friends and family understand the importance of digital privacy and how to safeguard their information online.

- **Campaign for Stronger Data Protection Laws:** Support policies that regulate data collection by governments and corporations, ensuring that privacy rights are upheld.

Foster Critical Thinking and Media Literacy

- **Develop Critical Analysis Skills:** Question narratives, identify biases, and consider the motives behind information presented by media and officials.

- **Promote Media Literacy Education:** Advocate for curricula in schools that teach students how to critically evaluate information sources and recognize propaganda or disinformation.

- **Engage in Constructive Dialogue:** Encourage open discussions that respect differing viewpoints, fostering a culture where questioning and healthy skepticism are valued.

Advocate for Ethical Technology

- **Support Ethical Tech Initiatives:** Choose products and services from companies that prioritize user privacy and ethical practices.

- **Participate in Public Consultations:** Engage in discussions about the implementation of new technologies, such as AI and surveillance tools, to ensure they are developed and used responsibly.

- **Collaborate with Technologists:** If you have expertise in technology, contribute to creating open-source tools that enhance transparency and protect privacy.

Build Community and Solidarity

- **Organize or Join Grassroots Movements:** Collective action amplifies individual voices. Participate in or create groups focused on issues like government transparency, human rights, and environmental protection.

- **Support Marginalized Communities:** Recognize that covert operations and unethical practices often disproportionately affect vulnerable populations. Advocate for policies that promote social justice and equality.

- **Encourage Ethical Leadership:** Vote for and support candidates who demonstrate integrity, transparency, and a commitment to democratic principles.

Legal Action and Advocacy

- **Use Legal Channels:** When witnessing unethical

or illegal activities, consider reporting them through appropriate legal channels. Seek legal counsel if necessary to protect yourself.

- **Support Legal Reforms:** Advocate for changes in laws that allow for excessive secrecy or unchecked power within government agencies and corporations.

- **Engage with International Bodies:** Support and engage with international organizations that monitor and address violations of human rights and democratic principles.

Reflection Exercise

Take a moment to reflect on your role in promoting transparency and accountability. Consider the following questions:

- **What steps can you take in your personal or professional life to support ethical practices and transparency?**

- **How can you contribute to creating a culture that values truth, critical thinking, and open dialogue?**

- **In what ways can you support those who risk their safety to expose injustices and unethical behavior?**

Call to Action

The shadows that conceal unethical practices thrive in environments of apathy and ignorance. By taking informed and deliberate action, each person has the power to contribute to a more transparent and just society. It begins with a commitment to stay informed, to question, and to stand up for democratic values. The illumination of truth is a collective effort let us each carry a light.

PART III: SUPPRESSED TECHNOLOGIES AND HIDDEN ADVANCES

CHAPTER 7:
SECRET SOCIETIES PEERING INTO THE SHADOWS CAST BY THE ILLUMINATI, FREEMASONS, AND OTHER HIDDEN POWERS

"The world is governed by very different personages from what is imagined by those who are not behind the scenes."
Benjamin Disraeli

Prologue

Throughout history, secret societies have intrigued, mystified, and terrified the public. From shadowy cabals that allegedly control world governments to fraternal organizations steeped in ancient rituals, these groups are often depicted as powerful forces manipulating global events from behind the scenes. Among the most notorious are the Illuminati, Freemasons, and other secretive organizations that have been blamed for everything from revolutions to economic crises. But what is the truth behind these secret societies? As historian Dr. Charles Whitmore delves into centuries-old manuscripts, hidden archives, and the whispered legends that surround these enigmatic groups, he uncovers a complex web of influence, power, and intrigue that continues to shape the world today. This chapter takes a deep dive into the world of secret societies, examining their origins, rituals, and the extent of their impact on historical and modern events.

The Illuminati: Guardians of Knowledge or Masters of Deception?

Perhaps the most famous and feared of all secret societies, the Illuminati have become synonymous with global conspiracy. Often depicted as a clandestine group of elites controlling governments, financial institutions, and cultural movements, the Illuminati's reputation is shrouded in myth and mystery.

Origins and the Bavarian Illuminati

- **The Founding of the Bavarian Illuminati**: The original Illuminati was founded on May 1, 1776, by Adam Weishaupt, a professor of canon law at the University of Ingolstadt in Bavaria, Germany. Weishaupt created the Illuminati as a secret society dedicated to enlightenment ideals, seeking to promote reason, secularism, and freedom from religious and state tyranny.

- **Goals and Structure**: The society was structured hierarchically, with members advancing through various degrees of initiation, each revealing deeper secrets and knowledge. The Illuminati sought to infiltrate influential positions within European governments, academia, and other societal institutions to spread their ideals.

- **The Suppression of the Illuminati**: In 1785, the Bavarian government banned the Illuminati, accusing them of subversion and plotting against the state. Many members were arrested, and the society was officially dissolved. However, rumors persisted that the Illuminati continued to operate in secret, expanding their influence across Europe and beyond.

Modern Conspiracy Theories and Alleged Influence

- **The Illuminati and the French Revolution**: Conspiracy theories about the Illuminati's involvement in world events began to flourish in the late 18th century. Some believe that the Illuminati played a key role in the French Revolution, orchestrating the downfall of the monarchy to advance their anti-monarchical agenda. The idea of a hidden hand manipulating the revolution added fuel to fears of a global conspiracy.

- **Influence on the Founding of the United States**: The United States, founded during the Age of Enlightenment, has often been linked to Illuminati symbolism. The presence of esoteric symbols, such as the All-Seeing Eye and unfinished pyramid on the U.S. dollar bill, has led some to speculate that the nation's founders were influenced, if not directly involved, with the Illuminati. Figures such as Thomas Jefferson and Benjamin Franklin, who were proponents of Enlightenment ideals, are frequently cited in these theories, although concrete evidence remains elusive.

- **Cultural Manipulation and Entertainment**: In the 20th and 21st centuries, the Illuminati's alleged influence has extended into popular culture, with claims that the group manipulates music, movies, and media to shape public opinion and promote specific agendas. High-profile celebrities are often accused of being members or pawns of the Illuminati, with symbolism supposedly hidden in music videos, film scripts, and public performances.

Symbols and Rituals

- **The All-Seeing Eye**: Perhaps the most recognized symbol associated with the Illuminati is the All-Seeing Eye, often depicted within a triangle. This symbol is said to represent knowledge, surveillance, and the Illuminati's omnipresent influence. While its origins predate the Illuminati and can be traced to various spiritual traditions, the symbol has become a shorthand for conspiracy theories about hidden control.

- **Secret Handshakes and Passwords**: Like many secret societies, the Illuminati were reputed to use secret signs, handshakes, and passwords to identify members and maintain secrecy. These clandestine rituals were designed to foster a sense of brotherhood and mutual recognition among initiates.

- **Occult Influences and Esoteric Teachings**: Some theories suggest that the Illuminati were not just politically motivated but were deeply involved in occult practices. Allegations of Satanic rituals, summoning spirits, and esoteric knowledge have fueled the perception of the Illuminati as not just a political group but a spiritual or even supernatural one.

The Modern Legacy of the Illuminati

- **Digital Age and Internet Culture**: The rise of the internet has breathed new life into Illuminati conspiracy theories. Online forums, YouTube videos, and social media platforms are rife with discussions and "evidence" of the Illuminati's continued influence. Memes, symbols, and coded messages are dissected and debated by millions of people worldwide, keeping the myth alive in the digital age.

- **Reality or Paranoia?**: Despite the widespread fascination, no conclusive evidence has ever been found to prove that the Illuminati, as popularly conceived, exists today. Historians generally agree that the original Bavarian Illuminati disbanded in the late 18th century, and modern theories are often seen as reflections of societal fears about power, secrecy, and loss of control rather than factual accounts.

Freemasonry: Builders of Civilization or Hidden Rulers?

The Freemasons are one of the oldest and most enduring fraternal organizations in the world. While their influence is often associated with charitable work and personal development, the Freemasons have long been accused of harboring secret agendas, manipulating political events, and controlling world affairs from behind the scenes.

The Origins and Growth of Freemasonry

- **Medieval Stone Masons to Modern Fraternity**: Freemasonry traces its origins back to the stonemasons' guilds of medieval Europe, which were responsible for building cathedrals, castles, and other monumental structures. Over time, these guilds evolved into a fraternal society dedicated to moral philosophy, spiritual development, and mutual support.

- **The Transition to Speculative Masonry**: By the 17th century, Freemasonry had transformed from an operative craft into a speculative fraternity, open to individuals from various professions who sought intellectual and spiritual enlightenment. Freemasonry's rituals, symbols, and teachings are steeped in allegory, drawing from the tools of stonemasonry to convey lessons about life, morality, and the search for truth.

- **Global Expansion and Influence**: Freemasonry rapidly spread across Europe and the Americas, attracting influential members, including politicians, military leaders, and intellectuals. The society's global reach and the prominent roles of its members in historical events fueled speculation about its influence on world affairs.

Rituals, Symbols, and Secret Knowledge

- **The Square and Compasses**: The most recognizable symbol of Freemasonry, the Square and Compasses, represents the balance between moral rectitude and spiritual guidance. The letter "G" often found in the symbol is said to represent God, Geometry, or the Great Architect of the Universe, emphasizing the Masonic belief in a higher power and the pursuit of knowledge.

- **Initiation Rites and Degrees**: Freemasonry is structured into degrees, each associated with specific teachings, symbols, and rituals. Initiates undergo elaborate ceremonies designed to impart moral lessons and test their commitment to the fraternity's values. The exact details of these rituals are closely guarded secrets, contributing to the aura of mystery surrounding the Masons.

- **Allegations of Occult Practices**: Freemasonry has been accused of harboring occult knowledge and engaging in rituals that draw on ancient mystical traditions. While Masons themselves typically deny any occult affiliations, the society's use of symbols, secret words, and esoteric teachings has fueled perceptions of hidden spiritual practices.

Influence on Historical Events

- **The American Revolution and Founding**

Fathers: Freemasonry played a significant role in the American Revolution, with many key figures, including George Washington, Benjamin Franklin, and Paul Revere, being active Masons. Masonic lodges served as meeting places where revolutionary ideas were discussed and disseminated, leading some to argue that Freemasonry was instrumental in the fight for independence.

- **The French Revolution and European Politics**: Freemasonry's influence extended to revolutionary movements across Europe, including the French Revolution. The society's emphasis on liberty, equality, and fraternity mirrored the revolutionary slogans of the time, leading to suspicions that Masonic lodges were hotbeds of radical thought and political plotting.

- **Modern Political Influence**: Freemasons have held prominent positions in governments, military, and business throughout modern history, leading to ongoing speculation about the extent of their influence. While some see Freemasonry as a benign force promoting ethical conduct and philanthropy, others view it as a network of elites conspiring to maintain control over global affairs.

Anti-Masonry and Persecution

- **Religious Opposition**: Freemasonry has long faced opposition from religious institutions, particularly the Catholic Church, which has condemned the society as heretical and incompatible with Christian teachings. Papal bulls issued in the 18th and 19th centuries forbade Catholics from joining the Freemasons, accusing them of subversion and blasphemy.

- **Political Suppression**: Freemasons have also been targeted by authoritarian regimes, including Nazi Germany, Fascist Italy, and Communist countries, which viewed the society as a threat to state control. Freemasons were persecuted, their lodges shut down, and their members arrested, reinforcing the perception that they were subversive agents of change.

- **Conspiracy Theories and Public Distrust**: Freemasonry's secretive nature and perceived influence have made it a target of countless conspiracy theories. Allegations of Masonic involvement in everything from assassinations to economic manipulation have contributed to a persistent undercurrent of suspicion and fear.

Other Secret Societies: The Web of Hidden Power

Beyond the Illuminati and Freemasons, numerous other secret societies have left their mark on history. From the Rosicrucians to Skull and Bones, these groups are often shrouded in mystery, with connections to influential figures and events that continue to fuel speculation about their true purpose.

The Rosicrucians: Mystics of the Renaissance

- **Origins and Beliefs**: The Rosicrucians emerged in the early 17th century as a secretive brotherhood dedicated to the pursuit of esoteric wisdom, alchemy, and spiritual enlightenment. Their manifestos, which appeared in Europe, spoke of hidden knowledge, the reformation of humanity, and the establishment of a utopian society.

- **Connection to Science and the Occult**: Rosicrucianism blended elements of mysticism, science, and philosophy, attracting scholars, alchemists, and early scientists. Figures such as Isaac Newton and Francis Bacon have been linked to Rosicrucian ideas, suggesting that the society played a role in the development of modern scientific thought.

- **Legacy and Influence**: Although the original Rosicrucian order's existence remains debated, its legacy continues in modern esoteric movements and secret societies that claim to carry on its teachings. The Rosicrucians are often seen as forerunners of the Enlightenment, advocating for a synthesis of mystical and rational thought.

Skull and Bones: The Power Behind the Ivy League

- **Origins at Yale University**: Skull and Bones, one of the most notorious collegiate secret societies, was founded at Yale University in 1832. The society, known for its elite membership and bizarre rituals, has been a breeding ground for influential figures in American politics, business, and intelligence.

- **Membership and Influence**: Notable members of Skull and Bones include former U.S. Presidents George H.W. Bush and George W. Bush, as well as numerous senators, judges, and business leaders. The society's emphasis on loyalty, secrecy, and networking has fueled accusations that Skull and Bones serves as a gateway to power for America's elite.

- **Rituals and Allegations**: Skull and Bones is infamous for its macabre rituals, including the alleged use of human skulls and other dark symbols. Critics accuse the society of fostering a culture of elitism, privilege, and hidden agendas that extend into the highest levels of government.

The Priory of Sion: Guardians of a Holy Secret

- **Myth or Reality?**: The Priory of Sion first gained public attention through the book *Holy Blood, Holy Grail*, which claimed that the society was a centuries-old order tasked with protecting the bloodline of Jesus Christ. According to this theory, the Priory's members include powerful European aristocrats and influential cultural figures.

- **Debunking and Controversy**: While much of the Priory's supposed history has been debunked as a modern fabrication, the legend persists in popular culture, thanks in part to works like Dan Brown's *The Da Vinci Code*. The idea of a secret group guarding hidden truths about religion and history continues to captivate imaginations.

- **Cultural Impact**: The allure of the Priory of Sion lies not in its factual basis but in the broader appeal of secret knowledge and hidden history. It represents the archetype of a secret society with the power to shape the world by controlling humanity's most sacred narratives.

Implications for Modern Society

The enduring fascination with secret societies reflects deep-seated fears about power, control, and the unseen forces that shape our world. While the reality of these organizations is often less sinister than the myths suggest, their influence both real and perceived raises important questions about transparency, accountability, and the nature of power.

The Psychology of Conspiracy

- **Why We Believe**: Conspiracy theories about secret societies tap into fundamental human anxieties about control, trust, and the unknown. In an increasingly complex and interconnected world, the idea that a hidden hand is guiding events offers a simple, if often misguided, explanation for chaos and uncertainty.

- **The Impact of Distrust**: Belief in secret societies and their hidden influence can erode trust in institutions, from governments to media. This distrust can have real-world consequences, fueling political polarization, social division, and even violence.

The Reality of Hidden Agendas

- **Hidden Power Structures**: While the more outlandish theories about secret societies may lack evidence, the existence of hidden power structures such as lobbying groups, intelligence agencies, and corporate networks demonstrates that secretive, self-interested entities do shape global events.

- **Accountability and Transparency**: The perception of hidden influence underscores the need for greater transparency and accountability in governance, business, and other areas of public life. Exposing and addressing real-world conspiracies, such as corruption or collusion, is essential to building public trust.

The Cultural Legacy of Secret Societies

- **Symbols and Rituals in Popular Culture**: Secret societies continue to inspire books, movies, and television shows, reflecting our fascination with the unknown. From *The Da Vinci Code* to *National Treasure*, these stories capture the allure of hidden knowledge and the quest for truth, even in a fictionalized form.

- **Lessons from the Past**: The history of secret societies offers lessons about the dangers of secrecy, the allure of power, and the need for vigilance against those who seek to manipulate events from behind the scenes. Understanding the real and imagined influence of these groups helps us navigate the complexities of the modern world.

Conclusion

Secret societies have long captured the public imagination, blending history, myth, and conspiracy into a potent mix of intrigue and fear. Whether as guardians of hidden knowledge, manipulators of world events, or simply misunderstood fraternal organizations, their legacy continues to shape how we perceive power and influence. By peering into the shadows cast by the Illuminati, Freemasons, and other hidden groups, we gain a deeper understanding of the forces that drive human history and the enduring desire to uncover the secrets of those who operate in the dark.

"In the end, the greatest secret of all may be that the power we fear lies not in hidden societies but in our own willingness to believe in them."
Dr. Charles Whitmore

Reflection Questions:

> **How have secret societies influenced the course of history, and what are the key factors that have fueled conspiracy theories about their power and control?**

> **What role does secrecy play in the functioning of these organizations, and how does it contribute to both their perceived influence and public mistrust?**

> **How can modern society balance the desire for transparency and accountability with the recognition that some level of secrecy and discretion is necessary in governance and business?**

CHAPTER 8: THE HIDDEN AGENDAS OF THE MODERN AGE COVERT OPERATIONS, SHADOW GOVERNMENTS, AND THE MANIPULATION OF WORLD EVENTS

"Behind every great fortune, there is a crime. Behind every world event, there is a hidden agenda."
Honoré de Balzac

Prologue

In the modern era, power is wielded not just in the open halls of governments and corporations but often behind closed doors, where decisions that shape the world are made in secret. Covert operations, shadow governments, and clandestine alliances are not just the stuff of spy novels they are real mechanisms used to manipulate political, economic, and social landscapes on a global scale. From covert military interventions to secret trade deals and the orchestration of coups, these hidden agendas reveal a darker side of international relations. Dr. Natalie Archer, a geopolitical analyst and former intelligence officer, delves into the labyrinth of secret operations, unclassified documents, and insider testimonies that expose the true extent of these hidden forces. This chapter explores the world of covert power, shining a light on the unseen hands that pull the strings of history.

Shadow Governments: The Unseen Power Behind the Throne

The concept of a "shadow government" refers to a network of influential individuals and groups that operate behind the scenes, wielding power outside the traditional structures of elected offices and public accountability. These entities, often composed of intelligence agencies, corporate interests, and elite political operatives, can steer the course of nations without public scrutiny.

The Deep State: Myth or Reality?

- **Defining the Deep State**: The term "Deep State" gained popularity as a way to describe a hidden network within governments that operates independently of elected officials, often acting in its own interests rather than those of the public. While the concept is most often associated with the United States, similar structures exist in many other countries, where entrenched bureaucracies, military hierarchies, and intelligence agencies wield significant influence.

- **Examples in History**: The idea of a shadow government

is not new. In ancient Rome, powerful senators and military leaders often manipulated the political system behind the scenes. In more recent history, examples include the Military-Industrial Complex in the U.S., which President Dwight D. Eisenhower famously warned against, highlighting the risk of unaccountable military and corporate alliances dictating foreign policy.

- **The Modern Deep State**: Today, the term Deep State is often used to describe the intertwining of intelligence agencies, defense contractors, and private corporations that influence government policies from the shadows. Critics argue that these entities have their own agendas, prioritizing profits, control, and the perpetuation of conflicts that justify their existence.

Operation Gladio: A Network of Secret Armies

- **Cold War Covert Networks**: During the Cold War, NATO countries established secret paramilitary units known as "stay-behind" armies, intended to resist potential Soviet invasions. Operation Gladio was the most infamous of these operations, involving clandestine forces that operated throughout Europe.

- **Links to Terrorism and Political Manipulation**: While ostensibly defensive, some elements of Gladio were implicated in false flag operations, bombings, and political assassinations. Documents and testimonies suggest that these secret armies were used not just to counter the Soviet threat but to manipulate domestic politics, discredit leftist movements, and maintain conservative power structures in Western Europe.

- **Revelations and Public Outcry**: The existence of Operation Gladio was officially confirmed in the 1990s, leading to public outrage in several

European countries. While governments initially denied involvement, declassified documents revealed a network of clandestine operatives and covert operations that had been concealed from public scrutiny for decades.

Continuity of Government and Emergency Powers

- **Secret Plans for Continuity**: In times of crisis, governments often activate contingency plans designed to ensure the continuity of leadership and national security. However, some of these plans grant extraordinary powers to unelected officials, enabling them to bypass normal checks and balances.

- **The Role of Secret Bunkers and Emergency Authorities**: During the Cold War, secret bunkers and command centers were constructed in various countries to house key government and military personnel in the event of a nuclear attack. These facilities, such as the Raven Rock Mountain Complex in the U.S., are equipped to operate autonomously, with systems in place to maintain control over military forces and communication networks.

- **Erosion of Civil Liberties**: The use of emergency powers can lead to the suspension of civil liberties, the imposition of martial law, and the concentration of authority in the hands of a few individuals. Critics argue that the potential for abuse is significant, as these measures often lack transparency and accountability.

Covert Operations: Shaping the World Through Deception

Covert operations are designed to influence events in ways that are not visible to the public, often involving espionage, disinformation, sabotage, and clandestine military actions. These operations can have profound and far-reaching effects on international relations, destabilizing regions and altering the course of history.

The CIA's Secret Wars

- **Regime Change and Coups**: The CIA has been involved in numerous covert operations to overthrow foreign governments perceived as hostile to U.S. interests. Notable examples include the 1953 coup in Iran that deposed Prime Minister Mohammad Mossadegh after he nationalized the oil industry, and the 1973 coup in Chile that ousted President Salvador Allende, leading to the dictatorship of Augusto Pinochet.

- **Covert Funding and Support**: Beyond direct intervention, the CIA has funded, armed, and trained insurgent groups, political parties, and paramilitary forces to influence outcomes in other nations. The Nicaraguan Contras in the 1980s and the Mujahideen in Afghanistan are examples of groups that received covert support as part of broader geopolitical strategies.

- **Operation Mockingbird: Media Manipulation**: During the Cold War, the CIA's Operation Mockingbird involved infiltrating major news organizations and using journalists as assets to spread propaganda. The program aimed to shape public perception and control the narrative around U.S. foreign policy, demonstrating the power of covert influence in shaping public opinion.

Russia's Hybrid Warfare and Disinformation Campaigns

- **Soviet Active Measures**: The Soviet Union pioneered the use of "active measures," a broad set of tactics including disinformation, subversion, and political warfare aimed at undermining adversaries from within. This included funding leftist movements, spreading false stories, and using propaganda to discredit Western governments.

- **Modern Russian Tactics**: In the 21st century, Russia has adapted these techniques to the digital age, employing hackers, trolls, and state-controlled media to influence elections, destabilize governments, and sow discord in Western democracies. The 2016 U.S. presidential election, Brexit, and other political movements have all been cited as targets of Russian disinformation campaigns.

- **Weaponizing Information**: The use of misinformation and cyber tactics by Russia exemplifies the new face of covert warfare, where digital tools are used to manipulate perceptions and erode trust in institutions. These strategies blur the line between war and peace, making traditional responses ineffective against such decentralized threats.

Covert Economic Warfare

- **Sanctions and Financial Manipulation**: Economic sanctions are a tool often used to pressure governments into compliance without resorting to military force. However, they can also serve as a form of economic warfare, destabilizing economies and punishing civilian populations while pursuing geopolitical goals.

- **The Role of Intelligence Agencies in Market Manipulation**: Intelligence agencies have been implicated in manipulating global markets, currencies, and commodities to gain strategic advantages. Operations that involve currency devaluation, stock market manipulation, and control of critical resources can have devastating effects on target nations, often with long-term repercussions.

- **Hidden Trade Wars and Secret Negotiations**: Behind the scenes, nations engage in trade wars and negotiate secret deals that shape global markets. These hidden conflicts often prioritize national or corporate interests over public welfare, creating imbalances that can lead to economic crises and political instability.

Clandestine Alliances and Secret Pacts

Throughout history, nations have forged secret alliances and pacts, often unbeknownst to their citizens, that dramatically influence geopolitical dynamics. These agreements can lead to wars, shifts in power, and the redrawing of borders, often with far-reaching and unforeseen consequences.

Secret Treaties and Alliances

- **The Molotov-Ribbentrop Pact**: One of the most infamous secret agreements was the non-aggression pact signed between Nazi Germany and the Soviet Union in 1939. Officially a peace agreement, the secret protocols of the Molotov-Ribbentrop Pact included plans to divide Eastern Europe into German and Soviet spheres of influence, setting the stage for World War II.

- **Yalta and the Division of Europe**: During World War II, Allied leaders met in secret to discuss the post-war division of Europe. The agreements made at Yalta and Potsdam laid the groundwork for the Cold War, dividing the continent into Western and Soviet spheres of influence. These clandestine decisions shaped the geopolitical landscape for decades, leading to conflicts and the division of nations.

- **The Sykes-Picot Agreement**: A secret treaty between Britain and France during World War I, the Sykes-Picot Agreement outlined the division of the Ottoman Empire's Middle Eastern territories. The arbitrary borders drawn by European powers ignored ethnic, religious, and cultural realities, sowing seeds of conflict that continue to plague the region to this day.

Modern Covert Alliances: Intelligence Sharing and Black Ops

- **Five Eyes and Intelligence Sharing**: The Five Eyes alliance, composed of the U.S., U.K., Canada, Australia, and

New Zealand, is one of the most extensive intelligence-sharing networks in the world. While officially focused on national security, the alliance has been involved in controversial surveillance programs that extend far beyond their original mandate, raising concerns about privacy and civil liberties.

- **The Black Budget and Secret Military Operations**: Governments allocate billions of dollars to classified projects and operations that are hidden from public oversight. Known as the "black budget," these funds are used for everything from covert military actions to secret technological research, often without accountability or transparency.

- **Special Forces and Clandestine Warfare**: Modern warfare increasingly relies on special operations forces that conduct missions in secret, often in countries where their presence is officially denied. These elite units engage in assassinations, sabotage, and training of local forces, influencing conflicts around the world while maintaining plausible deniability.

Hidden Agendas in International Organizations

- **The United Nations and Secret Diplomacy**: While the United Nations is often seen as a forum for international cooperation, much of its most influential work occurs behind closed doors. Powerful nations use backroom deals, bribes, and political pressure to advance their agendas, often at the expense of smaller countries.

- **IMF and World Bank: Economic Leverage**: The International Monetary Fund (IMF) and World Bank wield significant influence over developing nations through loans and financial aid, often attached to stringent conditions that dictate economic policy. Critics argue that these organizations serve as tools of Western economic dominance, enforcing neoliberal policies that prioritize debt repayment and austerity over social welfare.

- **The Bilderberg Group and Trilateral Commission**: These elite gatherings bring together world leaders, business moguls, and intellectuals to discuss global issues behind closed doors. While participants insist that the meetings are informal and non-binding, the secrecy surrounding these discussions has fueled speculation about their role in shaping world policies and maintaining the status quo.

Implications for Modern Society

The hidden agendas of covert operations, shadow governments, and clandestine alliances reveal a world where power often resides outside the reach of public scrutiny. These actions can undermine democratic institutions, destabilize regions, and manipulate global events in ways that are often detrimental to the public good.

The Erosion of Democracy and Accountability

- **The Threat to Open Governance**: The rise of secret operations and hidden power structures poses a fundamental challenge to democratic governance. When decisions are made in secret, without public oversight, the principles of accountability and transparency are eroded, undermining trust in institutions and leaders.

- **Surveillance State and Privacy Concerns**: The expansion of surveillance technologies and covert intelligence programs threatens individual privacy and civil liberties. Governments 'ability to monitor citizens without their knowledge raises serious ethical and legal questions about the balance between security and freedom.

The Risks of Escalation and Unintended Consequences

- **Blowback from Covert Actions**: Covert operations can have unforeseen and long-lasting consequences, often destabilizing regions and creating new threats. The funding of insurgent groups, for example, has frequently led to the emergence of extremist movements that turn against their former sponsors.

- **Manipulation of Public Perception**: The use of disinformation, propaganda, and media manipulation to shape public perception undermines the ability of citizens to make informed decisions. In an age of "fake news" and deepfakes, discerning truth from deception becomes increasingly difficult, exacerbating political polarization and social division.

The Future of Transparency and Reform

- **Demanding Greater Transparency**: Public pressure for greater transparency and accountability in government and international institutions is essential to countering the influence of hidden agendas. Whistleblowers, investigative journalists, and watchdog organizations play a crucial role in exposing covert operations and holding power to account.

- **Reforming Secretive Institutions**: Reforms aimed at increasing oversight of intelligence agencies, military operations, and economic institutions can help ensure that decisions are made in the public interest. Strengthening checks and balances, enhancing legislative oversight, and promoting open governance are key steps toward a more accountable system.

- **Embracing Technological Accountability**: As technology continues to evolve, new tools can be leveraged to increase transparency and accountability. Blockchain technology, for instance, offers potential applications for secure and transparent record-keeping, while AI-driven analysis can help detect and counteract disinformation campaigns.

Conclusion

The hidden agendas of the modern age reflect a world where power is often exercised in the shadows, with far-reaching consequences for individuals, nations, and the global order. Understanding the mechanisms of covert operations, shadow governments, and secret alliances is crucial to navigating the complexities of today's geopolitical landscape. By shining a light on these hidden forces, we can better protect democratic principles, promote accountability, and ensure that the actions taken in the name of security and progress truly serve the public good.

"The greatest danger to democracy is not the actions of hidden forces but the silence of those who know the truth and choose to look the other way."
Dr. Natalie Archer

Reflection Questions:

What are the key motivations behind covert operations and secret alliances, and how do these actions impact global stability and international relations?

How can modern societies protect democratic values and transparency in an age of covert influence and hidden agendas? What measures are needed to hold powerful institutions accountable?

How does the existence of shadow governments and clandestine operations shape public trust in leadership and institutions? How can this trust be rebuilt in an era of widespread disillusionment?

CHAPTER 9: TECHNOLOGY IN THE HANDS OF HIDDEN POWERS SURVEILLANCE, DATA MANIPULATION, AND THE BATTLE FOR CONTROL IN THE DIGITAL AGE

"Technology is a useful servant but a dangerous master. When controlled by hidden powers, it becomes the greatest threat to freedom in human history."
Prof. Jonathan Steele

Prologue

In the 21st century, technology has transformed every aspect of human life. From smartphones that connect us instantly to artificial intelligence that predicts our behavior, the digital age promises unprecedented convenience, efficiency, and knowledge. Yet, beneath the surface of this technological marvel lies a darker reality one where hidden powers exploit these tools to monitor, manipulate, and control populations on a global scale. Surveillance programs, data mining, and algorithmic bias are just a few of the ways technology is wielded as a weapon by those in power. Prof. Jonathan Steele, a former cybersecurity expert turned whistleblower, exposes the hidden mechanisms of control embedded in the technology we use every day. This chapter delves into the covert use of technology by governments, corporations, and clandestine groups, exploring how digital tools have become the new frontier in the battle for global dominance.

The Rise of the Surveillance State: Watching from the Shadows

Surveillance technology, once limited to military and intelligence applications, has now infiltrated every corner of society. Governments and corporations monitor our movements, communications, and even thoughts, turning the digital landscape into a vast panopticon where privacy is an illusion.

Mass Surveillance Programs: From PRISM to Pegasus

- **PRISM and the NSA's Global Reach**: The revelation of the PRISM program by whistleblower Edward Snowden in 2013 exposed the extent of global surveillance by the U.S. National Security Agency (NSA). PRISM allowed the NSA to collect data directly from tech giants like Google, Facebook, and Apple, including emails, messages, and phone records. The program was part of a broader effort to monitor global communications in the name of national security, but its scope and lack of oversight raised alarms about civil liberties and privacy.

- **Pegasus Spyware and Global Espionage**: Pegasus, developed by the Israeli cyber-intelligence firm NSO Group, is one of the most advanced spyware tools ever created. Capable of remotely hacking smartphones, Pegasus can access messages, calls, emails, and even turn on cameras and microphones without the user's knowledge. While marketed as a tool for fighting terrorism and crime, investigations revealed that Pegasus was used to target journalists, activists, and political opponents in multiple countries, highlighting the dangerous potential of surveillance technology in the wrong hands.

- **China's Social Credit System and AI Surveillance**: China has taken surveillance to unprecedented levels with its Social Credit System, which monitors citizens 'behavior and assigns scores based on their actions, including financial reliability, social interactions, and even online comments. AI-driven facial recognition cameras are ubiquitous in Chinese cities, tracking individuals' movements in real-time. This integration of surveillance into everyday life creates a system of control that rewards compliance and punishes dissent, effectively merging state power with technological oversight.

The Weaponization of Big Data

- **Data Mining and Predictive Analytics**: In the digital age, data is the new oil. Corporations and governments collect vast amounts of personal information, from purchasing habits to location data, which are then analyzed to predict and influence behavior. Predictive analytics, powered by AI and machine learning, are used to anticipate everything from consumer choices to political preferences, allowing those with access to data to shape markets and public opinion.

- **Cambridge Analytica and Election Manipulation**: The Cambridge Analytica scandal revealed how personal data harvested from millions of Facebook users was used to influence elections and political campaigns. By profiling individuals based on their data, Cambridge Analytica created targeted ads designed to exploit psychological vulnerabilities, manipulating public perception and potentially altering electoral outcomes. This case exposed the darker side of data analytics, where personal information becomes a tool for political warfare.

- **Corporate Surveillance and Consumer Profiling**: Beyond politics, data mining is used extensively by corporations to monitor and influence consumer behavior. Companies track every click, search, and purchase to build detailed profiles of their customers, which are then used to sell products, tailor advertising, and predict future behavior. While marketed as a way to enhance user experience, this constant monitoring also raises concerns about the commodification of privacy and the ethical implications of predictive marketing.

The Dark Web of Algorithmic Control

- **Algorithmic Bias and Social Engineering**: Algorithms govern much of the digital world, from search engine results to social media feeds. However, these algorithms are not neutral; they reflect the biases of their creators and the data they are fed. Algorithmic bias can lead to the amplification of misinformation, discrimination in hiring practices, and the creation of echo chambers that reinforce existing beliefs. The manipulation of algorithms by hidden powers can subtly shape public perception, fostering division and controlling narratives.

- **Social Media Manipulation and Fake News**: Social media platforms, designed to connect people, have become breeding grounds for misinformation, propaganda, and targeted manipulation. Bots, fake accounts, and deepfakes are used to spread false information, influence public opinion, and disrupt democratic processes. Governments, private companies, and even individuals can deploy these tools to manipulate reality, creating a post-truth environment where facts are malleable, and trust in information is eroded.

- **AI Policing and Predictive Crime**: Predictive policing algorithms, used by law enforcement agencies to forecast criminal activity, are often based on biased data that disproportionately targets marginalized communities. These systems can lead to over-policing of certain neighborhoods and perpetuate systemic inequalities. The use of AI in law enforcement raises ethical concerns about accountability, transparency, and the potential for abuse in the hands of corrupt or biased institutions.

Digital Warfare: The New Battlefield of Cyber Espionage and Hacking

As technology becomes increasingly integral to national security, cyber warfare has emerged as a critical front in modern conflicts. State-sponsored hackers, cyber-mercenaries, and rogue actors engage in a constant battle for control of information, infrastructure, and intelligence.

State-Sponsored Hacking and Cyber Espionage

- **The Shadow Brokers and the NSA's Cyber Arsenal**: In 2017, a mysterious group known as the Shadow Brokers released a trove of hacking tools developed by the NSA, including sophisticated exploits that targeted vulnerabilities in widely used software. These leaks exposed the extent of state-sponsored cyber capabilities and highlighted the risks of hoarding vulnerabilities that could be weaponized by malicious actors.

- **Russia's Cyber Operations and Election Meddling**: Russia has been at the forefront of using cyber operations as a tool of statecraft. From hacking the Democratic National Committee during the 2016 U.S. presidential election to launching ransomware attacks on critical infrastructure, Russian cyber tactics blend espionage, disinformation, and direct sabotage to achieve strategic objectives without conventional military engagement.

- **China's Cyber Espionage and Intellectual Property Theft**: China's cyber operations focus heavily on stealing intellectual property, trade secrets, and sensitive data from Western companies and governments. The use of sophisticated phishing campaigns, supply chain attacks, and advanced persistent threats allows Chinese hackers to infiltrate critical industries, from defense to pharmaceuticals, posing a significant threat to economic and national security.

The Rise of Cyber Mercenaries and Hack-for-Hire Groups

- **Hackers for Hire: Private Cyber Warfare**: Beyond state-sponsored actors, a growing market of cyber mercenaries offers hacking services to the highest bidder. These groups, often composed of former intelligence agents and rogue hackers, conduct espionage, ransomware attacks, and digital sabotage on behalf of corporations, governments, and criminal organizations. The privatization of cyber warfare blurs the line between nation-state and criminal activity, complicating efforts to attribute attacks and hold perpetrators accountable.

- **Ransomware and the Rise of Digital Extortion**:

Ransomware attacks, where hackers encrypt a victim's data and demand payment for its release, have become a lucrative business model for cybercriminals. High-profile attacks on hospitals, energy grids, and municipal governments demonstrate the vulnerability of critical infrastructure to digital extortion, raising concerns about the preparedness of public and private sectors to defend against these evolving threats.

- **Zero-Day Exploits and the Cyber Arms Race**: Zero-day exploits, vulnerabilities that are unknown to software developers and unpatched, are highly prized in the cyber world. These exploits can be sold on black markets for millions of dollars, fueling a cyber arms race where nations and hackers stockpile digital weapons. The use of zero-days in operations like Stuxnet, which targeted Iran's nuclear program, showcases the potential of cyber weapons to cause real-world damage.

Cyber Defense and the Quest for Digital Sovereignty

- **Protecting Critical Infrastructure**: As cyber threats evolve, defending critical infrastructure such as power grids, water systems, and communication networks has become a top priority for national security. Governments are investing heavily in cybersecurity measures, including the development of cyber command centers, AI-driven threat detection, and public-private partnerships to enhance resilience against attacks.

- **The Challenge of Attribution**: One of the biggest challenges in responding to cyberattacks is attributing the attack to its true source. The anonymity of the internet, combined with techniques like false flag operations and proxy hacking, allows attackers to mask their identity and evade accountability. This ambiguity complicates diplomatic responses and increases the risk of escalation in cyber conflicts.

- **The Future of Cyber Warfare**: As AI and quantum computing advance, the nature of cyber warfare is poised to change dramatically. Autonomous hacking tools, AI-driven disinformation campaigns, and quantum-based cryptography could redefine the battlefield, making cyber defense an even more complex and critical challenge. Nations that fail to keep pace with these technological developments risk falling victim to new forms of digital dominance.

The Ethics of Control: Technology, Freedom, and the Future

The covert use of technology to monitor, manipulate, and control populations raises profound ethical questions about the balance between security and freedom. As technology continues to evolve, so too does the potential for abuse, making it imperative to consider the moral implications of these powerful tools.

The Dangers of Technological Authoritarianism

- **The Rise of Digital Dictatorships**: In authoritarian regimes, technology is often used to suppress dissent, monitor citizens, and maintain power. From China's Great Firewall to the use of spyware against political opponents, digital tools are employed to create surveillance states where control is total and resistance is futile. The export of surveillance technology to other regimes further spreads this model, threatening global human rights.

- **Algorithmic Decision-Making and Social Control**: Algorithms increasingly influence decisions that affect people's lives, from loan approvals to job applications and legal judgments. When these algorithms are biased or designed with opaque criteria, they can perpetuate inequality and injustice. The lack of transparency and accountability in algorithmic governance poses a significant risk to democratic principles.

The Need for Digital Rights and Privacy Protections

- **Reclaiming Digital Sovereignty**: As technology becomes more pervasive, there is a growing movement to establish digital rights that protect individuals from invasive surveillance and data exploitation. Proposals for data privacy regulations, such as the European Union's General Data Protection Regulation (GDPR), aim to give citizens more control over their personal information and hold companies accountable for data breaches and misuse.

- **Balancing Security with Civil Liberties**: Governments face the challenge of balancing national security needs with the protection of civil liberties. Excessive surveillance and data collection can lead to abuses of power, but the absence of these measures can leave societies vulnerable to threats. Finding the right balance requires ongoing public debate, legal oversight, and robust checks on the use of surveillance technologies.

- **The Role of Whistleblowers and Activists**: Whistleblowers like Edward Snowden and activists advocating for digital privacy have played crucial roles in exposing abuses of surveillance and sparking global conversations about the ethical use of technology. Protecting those who speak out against injustices in the digital realm is essential to maintaining accountability and transparency.

The Future of Technology and Freedom

- **The Promise and Peril of AI**: Artificial intelligence holds the potential to revolutionize industries, enhance human capabilities, and solve complex problems. However, AI also poses risks of misuse, from autonomous weapons to deepfakes that undermine trust in information. Ensuring that AI development is guided by ethical principles and aligned with human values is critical to safeguarding the future.

- **Building Resilient Societies**: Resilience in the face of technological challenges requires not just technical solutions but a commitment to education, public awareness, and democratic engagement. Empowering individuals to understand, question, and influence the technologies that shape their lives is key to preventing the unchecked growth of digital authoritarianism.

Conclusion

The hidden powers that wield technology as a tool of surveillance, manipulation, and control represent a profound threat to freedom in the digital age. As society becomes increasingly intertwined with technology, the battle for control over these tools will shape the future of governance, privacy, and human rights. By confronting the ethical dilemmas posed by digital power and advocating for transparency, accountability, and digital sovereignty, we can work towards a world where technology serves humanity, rather than enslaving it.

"The question is not whether technology can be used to control us, but whether we will allow it to be. The future of freedom depends on our answers."
Prof. Jonathan Steele

Reflection Questions:

How can society strike a balance between the benefits of surveillance technology for security and the need to protect individual privacy and freedom?

What measures can be taken to ensure that AI and algorithmic decision-making are transparent, fair, and accountable? How can biases in these systems be addressed?

As technology evolves, what role should governments, corporations, and citizens play in shaping the ethical use of digital tools? How can we prevent the rise of digital authoritarianism?

CHAPTER 10: THE FINAL FRONTIER OF HIDDEN POWER MANIPULATING SCIENCE, SUPPRESSING REVOLUTIONARY DISCOVERIES, AND CONTROLLING THE FUTURE OF KNOWLEDGE

"The suppression of knowledge is the death of science, and the manipulation of discovery is the control of the future."
Dr. Evelyn Harrington

Prologue

Science has always been a beacon of human progress, pushing the boundaries of what is known and possible. Yet, beneath the surface of innovation lies a struggle for control over the direction of human knowledge. From the suppression of groundbreaking discoveries to the manipulation of research for political and financial gain, the scientific realm is not immune to the hidden agendas that shape the world. Dr. Evelyn Harrington, a prominent scientist and whistleblower, reveals how powerful forces manipulate science to maintain control over technological advancements and the future of humanity. This chapter explores the dark side of scientific discovery, uncovering how revolutionary breakthroughs are stifled, reshaped, or hidden from the public eye.

The Suppression of Revolutionary Discoveries: Hidden Science and Lost Innovations

Throughout history, certain scientific discoveries and technological innovations have been suppressed, often because they threatened powerful interests, challenged established paradigms, or offered disruptive solutions that would upend the status quo.

Energy Innovations: From Cold Fusion to Free Energy

- **Cold Fusion: The Forgotten Promise of Limitless Energy**
  In 1989, chemists Martin Fleischmann and Stanley Pons announced their discovery of cold fusion, a process that claimed to produce nuclear fusion at room temperature, promising an abundant and clean energy source. Despite initial excitement, the scientific community quickly dismissed their findings, citing issues with reproducibility and experimental errors. However, many believe that the potential of cold fusion was buried due to vested interests in the energy sector, fearing a technology

that could render fossil fuels obsolete. Today, cold fusion remains a controversial topic, with some researchers quietly continuing the work away from the public eye.

- **The Suppression of Nikola Tesla's Energy Technologies**
Nikola Tesla's work on wireless electricity, zero-point energy, and other advanced technologies has long been shrouded in mystery and suppression. Many of Tesla's patents were seized by the U.S. government upon his death, and much of his work was classified. Speculation persists that Tesla's innovations in energy could have provided the world with free and unlimited power, bypassing the need for traditional power grids and fossil fuels. However, his inventions were never fully realized, possibly due to the immense threat they posed to the established energy industry.

- **Magnetic Motors and Perpetual Motion Machines**
Inventors have long sought to create machines that could generate power with minimal or no input energy, often using magnets, gyroscopes, and unconventional designs. While mainstream science dismisses these devices as violating the laws of thermodynamics, persistent reports and patent filings suggest that some inventors have developed working prototypes. The suppression of such technologies is often attributed to powerful industries that stand to lose from the disruption of traditional energy models.

Medical Breakthroughs: Cures Suppressed for Profit

- **Cancer Cures and the Pharmaceutical Industry**
The search for a cure for cancer has been a major focus of medical research for decades, yet stories of suppressed cures abound. From alternative treatments using cannabinoids, laetrile (Vitamin B17), and natural compounds to unorthodox approaches like Gerson therapy and intravenous vitamin C, many promising

cancer treatments have been sidelined or discredited. Critics argue that the multi-billion-dollar cancer treatment industry prioritizes profit over cures, favoring ongoing treatments over one-time solutions.

- **Dr. Royal Rife and the Frequency Cure**
  In the 1930s, Dr. Royal Rife developed a machine that used specific frequencies to target and destroy cancer cells, reportedly achieving remarkable results. However, Rife's work was suppressed, and his laboratory was raided. His frequency technology was discredited by the medical establishment, and he died in obscurity. Today, Rife's machines are used by alternative health practitioners, but his story remains a cautionary tale of innovation crushed by powerful medical interests.

- **The Buried Potential of Stem Cell Therapies**
  Stem cell research offers the potential to regenerate damaged tissues, cure degenerative diseases, and even reverse aging. However, ethical controversies, regulatory restrictions, and the high cost of research have hindered the development and accessibility of stem cell treatments. Some promising therapies have been delayed or restricted by bureaucratic hurdles, often influenced by pharmaceutical companies that stand to lose from curative treatments that reduce the need for chronic medication.

Environmental and Agricultural Technologies

- **Suppressed Green Technologies: From Plastic-Eating Bacteria to Water-Powered Engines**
  As environmental crises mount, innovative solutions have emerged that could dramatically reduce pollution and resource consumption. Technologies such as plastic-eating bacteria, water-powered engines, and advanced recycling methods have been developed but are often suppressed or slow to reach the market due to resistance

from entrenched industries. For example, water-fueled engines, which use electrolysis to split water into hydrogen and oxygen as fuel, have been patented and then shelved, sparking conspiracy theories about oil companies buying and burying disruptive technologies.

- **Genetically Modified Organisms (GMOs) and the Control of Agriculture**
  The advent of genetically modified crops has revolutionized agriculture, but it has also concentrated control in the hands of a few biotech giants. These companies patent genetically engineered seeds, requiring farmers to purchase new seeds each season rather than saving them, as has been done for millennia. Allegations of health risks, environmental damage, and economic exploitation have fueled debates about the ethical implications of GMOs. Critics argue that these technologies are used not just to increase yields but to dominate global food production, prioritizing profits over ecological and human health.

- **Permaculture and Regenerative Agriculture**
  Alternative agricultural models like permaculture and regenerative farming offer sustainable solutions that can restore soil health, increase biodiversity, and reduce reliance on chemical inputs. However, these practices are often marginalized in favor of industrial agriculture, which is heavily subsidized and controlled by large agribusiness corporations. The suppression of sustainable farming practices underscores the broader struggle for control over the future of food.

The Manipulation of Scientific Research: Control Over the Narrative

Science is often portrayed as an objective pursuit of truth, but in reality, research is subject to manipulation by funding sources, political pressures, and institutional biases. This manipulation can shape public perception, guide policy decisions, and determine which technologies and discoveries are brought to light.

The Funding Game: Who Pays, Who Decides

- **Corporate Sponsorship and Research Bias**
  Much of scientific research is funded by private corporations, which often have a vested interest in the outcomes. Pharmaceutical companies, for example, fund studies on their own drugs, leading to conflicts of interest that can skew results. Research that produces unfavorable findings may be suppressed, delayed, or discredited, while studies that align with corporate goals are promoted. This dynamic creates a biased research landscape where certain lines of inquiry are encouraged, and others are discouraged or ignored.

- **Government Influence and Classified Research**
  Governments also play a significant role in directing scientific research, often with national security or strategic interests in mind. Research related to advanced energy, military technology, and other sensitive areas is frequently classified, limiting public access to potentially transformative discoveries. Military research into areas like directed energy weapons, quantum computing, and bioengineering is often conducted in secrecy, with breakthroughs shielded from public and commercial use.

- **Academic Pressure and the Publish-or-Perish Paradigm**
  The pressure on academics to publish frequently can lead to compromised research quality, selective reporting, and the replication crisis, where many published findings cannot be reproduced. Researchers may avoid pursuing unconventional or controversial topics that could jeopardize funding or tenure, reinforcing the status quo and stifling innovative thinking.

Scientific Consensus and the Gatekeepers of Knowledge

- ### The Role of Peer Review and Academic Journals
  Peer review is designed to ensure the quality and validity of scientific research, but it can also serve as a gatekeeping mechanism that suppresses unconventional ideas. Innovative research that challenges established theories may struggle to find publication, particularly if it contradicts the interests of influential reviewers or editors. This can create an environment where only certain viewpoints are validated, and alternative theories are sidelined.

- ### The Suppression of Climate Science and Environmental Research
  Environmental research, particularly related to climate change, has faced significant pushback from powerful industries, including fossil fuels and agriculture. Efforts to downplay or discredit findings that highlight environmental degradation, global warming, and biodiversity loss are often backed by well-funded lobbying campaigns. Scientists who speak out about these issues can face harassment, funding cuts, and professional ostracism, illustrating the high stakes of environmental advocacy.

- ### The Influence of Think Tanks and Policy Institutes
  Think tanks and policy institutes often shape public discourse on scientific issues, but many are funded by corporations, political parties, or wealthy individuals with specific agendas. These organizations produce research, white papers, and policy recommendations that reflect their sponsors 'interests, influencing legislation and public opinion. The line between independent scholarship and advocacy is often blurred, complicating the public's ability to discern unbiased information.

Scientific Skepticism and the Dangers of Dismissal

- **Ridicule of Fringe Science and Unorthodox Theories**
  Scientific communities are often skeptical of fringe theories, dismissing them as pseudoscience or quackery. While skepticism is an essential part of scientific inquiry, it can also lead to the premature dismissal of unconventional ideas that later prove to have merit. The initial ridicule faced by pioneers like Ignaz Semmelweis, who promoted handwashing in hospitals, or Alfred Wegener, who proposed continental drift, serves as a reminder of how transformative ideas can be resisted by the mainstream.

- **The Role of Debunkers and Professional Skeptics**
  Professional skeptics, often backed by industry or ideological groups, actively work to debunk unconventional theories and alternative practices. While this scrutiny is valuable for maintaining scientific standards, it can also be weaponized to discredit emerging research that threatens established interests. Debunking campaigns often focus on undermining credibility rather than engaging with the evidence, perpetuating a cycle of suppression and control.

- **The Internet and the Spread of Alternative Science**
  The internet has democratized access to information, allowing alternative scientific theories and suppressed knowledge to reach a global audience. However, this openness also creates a fertile ground for misinformation, making it difficult to distinguish credible science from baseless claims. The struggle between mainstream science and alternative narratives plays out online, influencing public perception and challenging traditional gatekeepers of knowledge.

Controlling the Future: The Battle for Technological Dominance

As science and technology advance, the race to control the future becomes increasingly intense. From artificial intelligence to genetic engineering, the technologies of tomorrow hold the power to reshape society, economies, and even human evolution. Those who control these technologies will shape the world in their image, raising profound ethical questions about who decides the future of humanity.

Artificial Intelligence: The New Arms Race

- **AI Supremacy and the Quest for Digital Dominance**
  Nations are competing fiercely for leadership in artificial intelligence, a technology that promises to revolutionize everything from warfare to healthcare. AI-driven systems can enhance national security, automate industries, and provide strategic advantages, but they also pose risks of job displacement, bias, and loss of human autonomy. The race for AI supremacy is not just about technological innovation; it is a struggle for global power.

- **Ethical Dilemmas in AI Development**
  As AI becomes more integrated into society, ethical concerns about surveillance, data privacy, and algorithmic bias come to the forefront. Decisions made by AI systems can have far-reaching consequences, yet these systems are often developed without public input or oversight. The lack of transparency in AI development raises questions about accountability and the potential for abuse.

- **The Rise of Autonomous Weapons**
  Military applications of AI, including autonomous drones and robotic soldiers, represent a new frontier in warfare. The deployment of AI-driven weapons that can make life-and-death decisions without human intervention challenges existing norms of war and international law. The development of autonomous weapons is often shrouded in secrecy, leaving the public largely unaware of

the ethical and strategic implications.

Genetic Engineering and the Future of Humanity

- **CRISPR and the Genetic Revolution**
  The advent of CRISPR gene-editing technology has opened up new possibilities for genetic modification, from curing genetic diseases to enhancing human traits. While the potential benefits are enormous, the ethical dilemmas are equally profound. Who gets to decide what genetic modifications are permissible? How will access to genetic enhancements be regulated? The ability to rewrite the code of life raises questions about eugenics, inequality, and the definition of what it means to be human.

- **Biotechnology and the Control of Life**
  The control over genetic technologies extends beyond humans to animals, plants, and microorganisms. Biotechnology companies are patenting genetically modified organisms, creating monopolies over life forms that have significant implications for agriculture, medicine, and environmental management. The commercialization of genetic information raises ethical concerns about the commodification of life itself.

- **Biosecurity and the Risk of Genetic Manipulation**
  Advances in genetic engineering also bring risks, including the potential for bioterrorism, accidental releases, and unintended ecological impacts. The dual-use nature of biotechnology capable of both beneficial and harmful applications makes biosecurity a critical issue. Controlling who has access to genetic engineering tools and how they are used will be a defining challenge of the coming decades.

The Fight for Control Over the Future of Science

- **The Privatization of Space Exploration**
  Space, once the domain of national governments,

is increasingly dominated by private companies. Entrepreneurs like Elon Musk, Jeff Bezos, and Richard Branson are leading the charge in commercial space travel, asteroid mining, and the colonization of other planets. While their ventures are celebrated as pioneering, they also raise questions about the privatization of space and the potential for a new era of colonialism beyond Earth.

- **Nanotechnology and the Control of the Microscopic World**

Nanotechnology, the manipulation of matter on an atomic scale, has vast potential applications in medicine, manufacturing, and environmental cleanup. However, the unknown risks of nanoparticles, including toxicity and environmental impact, pose significant challenges. The race to develop nanomaterials is another battleground for technological dominance, with implications for health, safety, and global power dynamics.

- **Quantum Computing: The Ultimate Game Changer**

Quantum computing promises to revolutionize information processing, solving complex problems far beyond the capabilities of classical computers. This technology could break current encryption methods, rendering traditional cybersecurity measures obsolete and reshaping fields from cryptography to artificial intelligence. Control over quantum computing could redefine economic and military power, making it a critical focus of scientific competition.

Conclusion

The manipulation of science and the suppression of revolutionary discoveries are not just historical footnotes they are ongoing struggles that shape the present and future of humanity. As powerful interests vie for control over the next great technological breakthroughs, the need for transparency, ethical oversight, and public engagement has never been greater. The future of knowledge belongs to those who dare to challenge the status quo, push the boundaries of what is known, and defend the integrity of science against those who seek to control it.

"The true frontier of discovery is not the unknown, but the battle to keep knowledge free from the hands of those who would wield it as a weapon."
 Dr. Evelyn Harrington

Reflection Questions:

> How can society ensure that scientific research and technological innovation are conducted ethically, transparently, and in the public interest?

> What are the implications of allowing private corporations and governments to control the development and deployment of advanced technologies? How can we democratize access to scientific knowledge?

> As new technologies emerge, what measures can be taken to balance innovation with the need for regulation, safety, and ethical considerations?

PERSONAL REFLECTIONS AND TESTIMONIES

The Lost Inventions: A Scientist's Struggle Against Suppression

By Dr. Jonathan Hayes

As a physicist specializing in alternative energy sources, I devoted my career to exploring innovative solutions to the world's growing energy demands. My journey began with a simple question: Could there be untapped sources of energy that defy conventional understanding? This quest led me down a path filled with groundbreaking discoveries, unexpected alliances, and formidable obstacles.

In the early years of my research, I stumbled upon the work of Nikola Tesla, whose visionary ideas about wireless energy transmission and zero-point energy captivated me. Inspired, I embarked on experiments to harness what is often referred to as "free energy" energy that could be extracted from the fabric of space itself.

After years of experimentation, my team and I developed a prototype device capable of generating electricity without any conventional fuel source. The implications were staggering a clean, inexhaustible energy supply that could revolutionize society. Eager to share our findings, we applied for patents and sought partnerships to bring the technology to market.

However, our excitement was short-lived. We encountered unexpected resistance from patent offices, which delayed and ultimately rejected our applications on ambiguous grounds. Potential investors withdrew without explanation, and we received veiled warnings to abandon our project. It became clear that powerful interests were intent on suppressing our work.

Undeterred, we decided to publish our research openly, believing that transparency would protect us and benefit humanity. Shortly after, we faced legal challenges alleging that our technology infringed on existing patents held by major energy corporations claims that were baseless but financially draining to contest.

Simultaneously, we experienced unusual setbacks: laboratory break-ins, data theft, and funding sources mysteriously drying up. Colleagues distanced themselves, fearing association with a controversial endeavor. The combined pressure was immense, forcing us to halt our work.

The most disheartening moment came when I received an offer from a representative of an unnamed organization. They proposed a substantial sum for exclusive rights to our technology, with the stipulation that we cease all further development and remain silent about our findings. The implication was clear: our invention would be buried.

Faced with a moral dilemma, I refused the offer. Instead, I took a different route collaborating with like-minded scientists globally to share knowledge and advance open-source energy solutions. We formed a network dedicated to pursuing suppressed technologies, supporting each other against external pressures.

While progress is slow and challenges persist, I remain hopeful. The experience revealed the lengths to which certain entities will go to maintain control over energy resources. Yet, it also illuminated the resilience and ingenuity of those committed to positive change. I believe that transparency, collaboration, and persistence will eventually bring these hidden advances to light.

The Healer's Discovery: Unlocking Alternative Medicine

By Dr. Maya Patel

As a medical doctor trained in Western medicine, I initially held a skeptical view of alternative healing modalities. My perspective shifted dramatically after a personal health crisis. Diagnosed with a chronic autoimmune condition, I found limited relief through conventional treatments. Desperate for solutions, I explored complementary therapies, including acupuncture, herbal medicine, and energy healing.

To my astonishment, these approaches led to significant improvements in my condition. Intrigued, I delved into studying traditional healing systems from around the world Ayurveda, Traditional Chinese Medicine, and indigenous practices. I discovered that these systems offered profound insights into health and wellness, emphasizing balance, prevention, and the interconnectedness of body, mind, and spirit.

Eager to integrate these modalities into my practice, I pursued additional certifications and began offering patients a holistic approach to healthcare. Many responded positively, experiencing benefits where conventional medicine had failed.

However, I soon faced resistance from regulatory bodies and professional associations. I received warnings about promoting "unverified" treatments and was subjected to audits and reviews. Pharmaceutical representatives, once frequent visitors, began expressing concern over my reduced prescription rates. Subtle pressures mounted to conform strictly to established medical protocols.

The most alarming incident occurred when I was approached by a representative from a major pharmaceutical company. They offered funding for my clinic in exchange for prioritizing certain medications and discontinuing alternative treatments. The underlying message was clear: the integration of holistic therapies threatened their profit margins.

Recognizing the ethical implications, I declined the offer. Shortly after, I faced increased scrutiny, negative reviews, and even threats to revoke my medical license. It became evident that powerful interests were invested in suppressing alternative healing modalities to protect their financial stakes in the healthcare industry.

In response, I joined forces with other practitioners committed to holistic health. We established a coalition to advocate for integrative medicine, conduct research, and educate the public about the benefits of combining traditional and modern approaches.

The journey has been challenging, but the positive outcomes for patients reinforce the importance of this work. I believe that embracing a more comprehensive understanding of health can lead to better outcomes and empower individuals to take charge of their well-being.

The Innovator's Dilemma: Renewable Energy and Corporate Roadblocks

By Emily Chen

As an environmental engineer, I was passionate about developing sustainable energy solutions. After years of research, my team and I designed an innovative solar panel system with significantly higher efficiency than existing models. Our technology had the potential to make renewable energy more accessible and affordable.

We secured patents and sought partnerships with manufacturers and energy providers. Initial responses were enthusiastic, and we received interest from international investors. However, as we moved closer to commercialization, obstacles emerged.

Key meetings were abruptly canceled, investors withdrew without explanation, and regulatory hurdles appeared unexpectedly. We discovered that major players in the fossil fuel industry had acquired companies we were negotiating with, effectively blocking our progress.

Undeterred, we considered producing the panels independently. However, we faced legal challenges alleging infringement on vague patents held by conglomerates with deep pockets. The litigation costs threatened to bankrupt our startup.

Simultaneously, a disinformation campaign surfaced online, casting doubt on the effectiveness and safety of our technology. It was a coordinated effort to undermine our credibility and deter potential customers and partners.

Realizing the magnitude of opposition, we pivoted our strategy. We released our designs and research into the public domain, adopting an open-source model. By empowering communities and smaller enterprises to develop and adapt the technology, we aimed to bypass the corporate gatekeepers.

The response was inspiring. Grassroots movements embraced the technology, adapting it for local needs and contributing improvements. Collaborative networks formed globally, advancing renewable energy innovations beyond what we could have achieved alone.

While we sacrificed potential profits, the widespread adoption of our technology fulfilled our primary goal promoting sustainable energy. This experience highlighted the systemic barriers innovators face when challenging entrenched industries, but it also demonstrated the power of collective action and open collaboration.

PRACTICAL APPLICATIONS AND ACTION STEPS

Harnessing Hidden Advances: Empowering Individuals and Communities

The suppression of transformative technologies and advancements poses significant challenges. However, collective awareness and proactive efforts can help bring these innovations to light and integrate them into society. Here are practical steps to engage with suppressed technologies and promote their development.

Educate Yourself and Others

- **Research Alternative Technologies:** Explore credible sources that discuss suppressed technologies, such as documentaries, books, and scientific publications. Authors like Steven M. Greer and Tom Bearden provide insights into this field.

- **Stay Informed on Innovations:** Follow developments in alternative energy, holistic medicine, and emerging technologies through reputable journals and conferences.

- **Share Knowledge:** Host community discussions, workshops, or online forums to share information and stimulate interest in hidden advances.

Support Open-Source Initiatives

- **Contribute to Open Projects:** Participate in or donate to open-source projects focused on alternative technologies, such as open-source energy devices or software platforms promoting transparency.

- **Collaborate and Innovate:** Use your skills to improve upon existing designs, share ideas, and collaborate with others globally to advance technology democratically.

Advocate for Policy Changes

- **Lobby for Transparency:** Contact legislators to advocate for declassification of suppressed patents and increased transparency in government and corporate research.

- **Promote Renewable Energy Policies:** Support policies that incentivize renewable energy adoption, research funding, and infrastructure development.

- **Encourage Integrative Medicine:** Advocate for the recognition and integration of alternative healing modalities within healthcare systems.

Engage in Ethical Consumerism

- **Support Ethical Companies:** Purchase products from companies committed to sustainability, transparency, and innovation in alternative technologies.

- **Invest Responsibly:** If you invest, consider socially responsible investment funds that prioritize companies developing clean energy and ethical technologies.

- **Reduce Dependency on Fossil Fuels:** Incorporate renewable energy solutions into your home or community, such as solar panels, to decrease reliance on conventional energy sources.

Empower Community Initiatives

- **Community Energy Projects:** Collaborate with

neighbors to establish local renewable energy projects, such as community solar gardens or wind turbines.

- **Health and Wellness Programs:** Promote and participate in community programs that offer holistic health services, workshops, and education.

- **Local Innovation Hubs:** Support or create makerspaces and innovation labs where people can experiment with alternative technologies and share resources.

Protect and Encourage Innovators

- **Support Whistleblowers:** Advocate for stronger protections for individuals who expose suppression of technologies or unethical practices.

- **Mentor and Fund Innovators:** Offer mentorship, resources, or financial support to inventors and researchers working on breakthrough technologies.

- **Create Networks:** Establish or join networks that connect innovators with legal, technical, and financial assistance to navigate challenges.

Practice Holistic Health

- **Explore Alternative Therapies:** Incorporate practices like acupuncture, meditation, herbal remedies, and energy healing into your wellness routine.

- **Educate on Integrative Medicine:** Share information about the benefits of combining conventional and alternative therapies for comprehensive health care.

- **Support Practitioners:** Choose healthcare providers who offer integrative approaches and advocate for their inclusion in mainstream healthcare.

Foster Critical Thinking and Skepticism

- **Question Mainstream Narratives:** Analyze media and

industry messages critically, especially those dismissing alternative technologies without substantive evidence.

- **Encourage Open Dialogue:** Promote discussions that consider multiple perspectives on technology and innovation.

- **Support Independent Research:** Back institutions or groups conducting unbiased research into alternative technologies and therapies.

Utilize Legal Channels

- **Patent Reform Advocacy:** Support reforms that prevent the misuse of patents to suppress innovation.

- **Legal Aid for Innovators:** Provide or support access to legal assistance for those facing unjust legal challenges.

- **Regulatory Engagement:** Participate in public comment periods for regulatory changes affecting technology development and healthcare practices.

Cultivate Environmental Stewardship

- **Sustainable Living Practices:** Adopt habits that reduce environmental impact, such as conserving energy, recycling, and using sustainable products.

- **Environmental Education:** Educate others about the importance of sustainability and the role of suppressed technologies in environmental solutions.

- **Participate in Conservation Efforts:** Engage in local conservation projects and support organizations dedicated to protecting natural resources.

Reflection Exercise

Reflect on how suppressed technologies and hidden advances impact your life and the broader society. Consider these questions:

- **What technological or medical advancements are you curious about, and how might they benefit you or your community?**

- **How can you contribute to the development or dissemination of alternative technologies and practices?**

- **In what ways can you support innovators and practitioners who face challenges in bringing new ideas to light?**

Call to Action

The potential benefits of suppressed technologies and hidden advances are immense, offering solutions to pressing global challenges. By taking informed and collective action, individuals and communities can help uncover these innovations and integrate them into mainstream society. Your engagement is crucial whether through education, advocacy, or direct participation, you can play a part in shaping a future where knowledge and technology serve the greater good.

Final Thoughts

The exploration of suppressed technologies reveals not only the obstacles faced by innovators but also the resilience and ingenuity of those committed to progress. The testimonies shared highlight the complex interplay between power, profit, and the pursuit of knowledge. They remind us that vigilance, collaboration, and a steadfast dedication to ethical principles are essential in overcoming barriers to advancement.

As we continue our journey through the Forbidden Secrets of Humanity, may we be inspired to seek out hidden truths, support one another in our endeavors, and strive towards a world where innovation is nurtured and shared for the benefit of all.

PART IV: ESOTERIC KNOWLEDGE

CHAPTER 11: ESOTERIC KNOWLEDGE DECODING SYMBOLS, SACRED GEOMETRY, AND THE HIDDEN LANGUAGE THAT CONNECTS US TO THE COSMOS

"The universe speaks in a language of symbols, a sacred geometry that connects all things. To decode this hidden language is to unlock the secrets of existence itself."
Dr. Helena Armitage

Prologue

Throughout history, humans have sought to understand the

mysteries of existence through symbols, sacred geometry, and esoteric knowledge passed down through secret societies, ancient texts, and hidden traditions. This hidden language is not just the domain of mystics and philosophers but also a code embedded in art, architecture, and nature itself. From the Great Pyramid of Giza to the enigmatic crop circles that dot fields around the world, symbols and geometry whisper the secrets of the cosmos, inviting us to look beyond the material world and glimpse the deeper truths that govern reality. Dr. Helena Armitage, a renowned symbologist and historian, guides us through the complex tapestry of esoteric knowledge, revealing how ancient wisdom connects us to the cosmos and how decoding these symbols can transform our understanding of the universe.

The Power of Symbols: The Hidden Language of the Universe

Symbols are one of the most ancient and universal forms of communication, transcending language and culture. They serve as powerful tools that convey complex ideas, spiritual truths, and cosmic principles through simple forms. From sacred symbols like the Ankh and the Yin-Yang to modern-day emblems like corporate logos, symbols resonate with hidden meanings that connect us to the collective unconscious.

Ancient Symbols and Their Meanings

- **The Flower of Life: The Blueprint of Creation**
  The Flower of Life is a geometric pattern consisting of overlapping circles that form a flower-like design. Found in temples, manuscripts, and sacred sites around the world, it is considered one of the most ancient symbols of sacred geometry. The Flower of Life is believed to represent the blueprint of the universe, embodying the fundamental forms of space, time, and consciousness. It is often associated with the creation process and is thought to hold the key to understanding the

interconnectedness of all living things.

- **The Ankh: The Key of Life**
The Ankh, a cross with a loop at the top, is one of the most recognizable symbols of ancient Egypt. Often depicted in the hands of gods and pharaohs, the Ankh represents eternal life, fertility, and the union of male and female principles. It is sometimes called the "Key of Life" and is seen as a symbol of spiritual transformation and the life force that flows through the universe.

- **The Ouroboros: The Eternal Cycle of Renewal**
The Ouroboros, a serpent or dragon eating its own tail, is a symbol that appears in many ancient cultures, including Egyptian, Greek, and Norse mythology. It represents the cycle of life, death, and rebirth, as well as the eternal nature of the universe. The Ouroboros embodies the concept of infinity, unity, and the interconnectedness of all things, reminding us that creation and destruction are part of the same cosmic process.

- **The Yin-Yang: Balance and Duality**
The Yin-Yang symbol, originating from Chinese philosophy, represents the duality of existence light and dark, masculine and feminine, active and passive. It conveys the idea that opposites are interconnected and interdependent, constantly transforming into one another. The symbol serves as a reminder of the balance that exists within all aspects of life and the universe, illustrating the harmony that arises from the interplay of opposing forces.

Symbols in Sacred Architecture

- **The Great Pyramid of Giza: A Symbol of Cosmic Order**
The Great Pyramid of Giza is not only a marvel of engineering but also a monumental symbol of esoteric knowledge. Its precise alignment with the cardinal

points, the Golden Ratio proportions, and its possible astronomical alignments suggest that it was built as a reflection of cosmic order. The pyramid's design incorporates advanced mathematical principles and hidden chambers that many believe were intended to serve as initiation spaces, connecting initiates to the stars and the divine.

- **The Gothic Cathedrals: Geometry as Divine Expression** Medieval Gothic cathedrals, such as Notre-Dame in Paris and Chartres Cathedral, are masterpieces of sacred architecture infused with esoteric symbolism. The intricate stained glass windows, labyrinths, and rose windows are not mere decoration but serve as visual representations of the cosmos, spiritual teachings, and the path to enlightenment. These structures were designed according to sacred geometric principles, reflecting the belief that geometry was a divine language that could bridge the human and the divine.

- **Stone Circles and Megaliths: Portals to Other Realms** Ancient stone circles, like Stonehenge and the Carnac Stones in France, are shrouded in mystery and continue to intrigue researchers with their precise astronomical alignments and potential ritualistic functions. These megalithic structures were often positioned to align with solar, lunar, and stellar events, suggesting that they were used as calendars, observatories, or places of spiritual significance. Some esoteric traditions believe these sites act as portals or energy centers, connecting the earth to the cosmos.

Modern Symbols: Hidden in Plain Sight

- **Corporate Logos and the Power of Subconscious Influence** Symbols are not confined to ancient times; they permeate modern life in the form of corporate logos, advertising, and branding. Many of these logos incorporate esoteric symbols, such as the all-seeing eye, pentagrams, and suns, subtly influencing consumer behavior and perceptions. The deliberate use of these symbols suggests an understanding of their power to communicate on a subconscious level, tapping into archetypal energies that resonate deeply with the human psyche.

- **The All-Seeing Eye and the Pyramid**
  The All-Seeing Eye, often depicted within a pyramid, is a symbol that appears on the U.S. dollar bill and is frequently associated with conspiracy theories about secret societies like the Illuminati. Historically, the All-Seeing Eye represents divine providence, spiritual insight, and the watchful eye of the cosmos. Its placement within the unfinished pyramid symbolizes the ongoing work of humanity's spiritual evolution, a process overseen by higher forces.

- **Pentagrams and Hexagrams: Symbols of Power and Protection**
  The pentagram, a five-pointed star, and the hexagram, a six-pointed star, are symbols that have been used throughout history in both protective and ritualistic contexts. The pentagram often represents the human body, the elements, and the balance between spirit and matter, while the hexagram, known as the Star of David or Seal of Solomon, symbolizes unity, balance, and the merging of opposites. Both symbols are used in esoteric traditions for their perceived power to invoke spiritual protection and connect with higher realms.

Sacred Geometry: The Mathematical Language of the Universe

Sacred geometry is the study of geometric patterns that underlie the structure of the universe, reflecting the belief that the cosmos is organized according to specific mathematical principles. From the spirals of seashells to the complex forms of galaxies, sacred geometry reveals the hidden order that connects all things.

The Platonic Solids: Building Blocks of Creation

- **The Five Platonic Solids**

  The Platonic Solids are five geometric shapes tetrahedron, cube, octahedron, dodecahedron, and icosahedron named after the Greek philosopher Plato, who associated each shape with a different element: fire, earth, air, ether, and water. These shapes are considered the building blocks of the physical world, embodying the principles of harmony, balance, and proportion. In esoteric traditions, the Platonic Solids are seen as the geometric blueprints of creation, representing the foundational forms that make up all matter.

- **Applications in Art and Architecture**

  The influence of the Platonic Solids extends beyond theoretical mathematics, appearing in art, architecture, and sacred spaces throughout history. The design of temples, cathedrals, and even modern structures often incorporates these geometric forms to evoke a sense of divine harmony and alignment with cosmic principles. Renaissance artists like Leonardo da Vinci and architects like Antoni Gaudí drew upon the principles of sacred geometry to infuse their works with spiritual resonance.

- **The Dodecahedron: A Portal to the Divine**

  The dodecahedron, associated with the element of ether, is often considered the most mystical of the Platonic Solids. Plato described it as the shape of the cosmos, and it has been linked to concepts of the divine, the etheric realm, and the fabric of the universe. Some esoteric traditions view the dodecahedron as a gateway to higher dimensions, representing the etheric energy that permeates all things.

The Golden Ratio: The Divine Proportion

- **Phi (Φ) and the Fibonacci Sequence**
  The Golden Ratio, denoted by the Greek letter Phi (Φ), is approximately 1.618 and is often found in nature, art, and architecture. The Fibonacci Sequence, a series of numbers where each number is the sum of the two preceding ones, is closely related to the Golden Ratio. As the sequence progresses, the ratio between successive numbers approximates Phi, reflecting a natural pattern of growth and harmony.

- **Nature's Hidden Code**
  The Golden Ratio is present in the spirals of shells, the branching of trees, the patterns of leaves, and the proportions of the human body. It is a recurring motif in the formation of galaxies, hurricanes, and even DNA. This universal constant reflects an underlying order that connects the microcosm to the macrocosm, suggesting that the same principles that govern the growth of a flower also shape the stars.

- **Sacred Art and the Golden Ratio**
  Artists and architects throughout history have used the Golden Ratio to create works that resonate with aesthetic and spiritual harmony. The Parthenon in Athens, the Great Pyramid of Giza, and Leonardo da Vinci's *Vitruvian Man* all incorporate the Golden Ratio, reflecting the belief that this divine proportion embodies perfection and beauty. In sacred art, the use of Phi is seen as a way to connect the viewer to the divine order of the cosmos.

The Vesica Piscis: The Womb of Creation

- **The Geometry of Duality and Unity**
  The Vesica Piscis, formed by the intersection of two circles, is a powerful symbol of duality, balance, and

creation. It is often associated with the union of opposites, such as male and female, heaven and earth, and spirit and matter. In Christian iconography, the Vesica Piscis is used to depict Christ and other holy figures, symbolizing the divine manifestation in the physical world.

- **Applications in Sacred Sites and Mystical Traditions**
  The Vesica Piscis appears in the architecture of cathedrals, mandalas, and the design of many sacred sites, reflecting its importance as a symbol of spiritual transformation and cosmic birth. In esoteric traditions, it is seen as the womb of creation, the space where the material and immaterial meet, giving rise to all forms of life. Its presence in sacred spaces is a reminder of the interconnectedness of all things and the unity underlying apparent duality.

- **The Tree of Life and the Flower of Creation**
  The Tree of Life, a central symbol in Kabbalistic mysticism, incorporates the Vesica Piscis within its geometric structure. This diagram represents the path of spiritual ascent, the journey from the physical realm to divine union. The intersections within the Tree of Life are often depicted as flowers or fruits, each representing a stage of enlightenment and cosmic understanding.

The Hidden Language of the Cosmos: Connecting with the Divine Through Symbol and Form

Esoteric knowledge suggests that symbols and sacred geometry are not just abstract concepts but are deeply connected to the very fabric of reality. They are thought to act as a bridge between the physical and spiritual realms, offering a way to communicate with the divine and understand the hidden laws that govern the universe.

Crop Circles: Messages from Beyond

- **The Mystery of Crop Circles**
Crop circles are intricate geometric patterns that appear mysteriously in fields, often overnight. While many are attributed to human pranksters, others display complex designs and mathematical precision that seem beyond human capability. Some researchers believe crop circles are a form of communication from higher intelligence, extraterrestrial beings, or interdimensional entities, conveying messages about cosmic order, environmental concerns, or spiritual awakening.

- **Sacred Geometry in Crop Circles**
Many crop circles incorporate elements of sacred geometry, such as the Flower of Life, the Vesica Piscis, and the Platonic Solids. These patterns often appear in alignment with ancient sacred sites, ley lines, or celestial events, suggesting a deliberate connection to the Earth's energy grid. The presence of these symbols reinforces the idea that crop circles are not random but are intentional designs with deeper meaning.

- **Scientific and Esoteric Interpretations**
Some scientists have explored the physical effects associated with genuine crop circles, such as changes in electromagnetic fields, soil composition, and plant structure. Esoteric interpretations suggest that crop circles are part of a larger phenomenon of Earth's awakening, acting as visual affirmations of the interconnectedness between humanity and the cosmos. Whether seen as art, message, or mystery, crop circles invite us to question the nature of reality and the forces that shape our world.

The Language of Light and Sound

- **Cymatics: The Sound of Creation**
Cymatics is the study of sound vibrations and their effects on physical matter. By using sound frequencies to vibrate

materials such as sand, water, or metal, intricate patterns and shapes emerge, revealing the power of sound to shape reality. These patterns often mirror the geometric forms found in sacred symbols, suggesting that sound is a fundamental force in the creation of the universe. Esoteric traditions, such as the chanting of sacred mantras, recognize the power of sound to heal, transform, and connect with the divine.

- **Light Language and Sacred Codes**
Light language, sometimes referred to as the language of the soul, is a form of non-linear communication that uses symbols, sounds, and gestures to convey spiritual truths and healing energies. Practitioners believe that light language bypasses the conscious mind, connecting directly with the soul and higher dimensions. It is thought to be an ancient form of communication used by advanced civilizations and celestial beings, offering a way to access esoteric knowledge and activate dormant spiritual DNA.

- **The Merkaba: A Vehicle of Light and Ascension**
The Merkaba, depicted as two interlocking tetrahedrons spinning in opposite directions, is a symbol of spiritual ascension and light body activation. In esoteric teachings, the Merkaba represents a vehicle of light that can transport consciousness between dimensions, offering protection, healing, and spiritual awakening. Meditating on the Merkaba or visualizing its form is believed to connect the individual to higher realms and facilitate spiritual growth.

Alchemical Symbols and the Transformation of Consciousness

- **The Philosophers 'Stone: The Ultimate Symbol of Transformation**
In alchemy, the Philosophers 'Stone is the legendary

substance that can turn base metals into gold and grant immortality. Beyond its literal interpretation, the stone symbolizes the inner alchemical process of spiritual transformation the transmutation of the self from ignorance to enlightenment. The search for the Philosophers 'Stone represents the quest for divine wisdom, self-realization, and the attainment of the eternal.

- **The Sacred Marriage: Union of Opposites**
The alchemical concept of the Sacred Marriage, or *coniunctio*, represents the union of opposing forces within the self masculine and feminine, spirit and matter, light and shadow. This symbolic marriage is the key to achieving the alchemist's goal of wholeness and enlightenment. The imagery of the alchemical wedding, often depicted as a king and queen embracing, symbolizes the reconciliation of dualities and the emergence of a higher state of consciousness.

- **The Emerald Tablet and the Hermetic Wisdom**
The Emerald Tablet, attributed to the mythical Hermes Trismegistus, is a foundational text of alchemical philosophy. Its most famous line, "As above, so below," encapsulates the principle that the microcosm reflects the macrocosm, and that the same laws govern both the seen and unseen realms. The tablet's cryptic verses are said to contain the secrets of the universe, offering a roadmap for spiritual transformation and the attainment of ultimate knowledge.

Conclusion

Esoteric knowledge, with its symbols, sacred geometry, and hidden language, invites us to look beyond the surface of reality and explore the deeper connections that bind the universe together. These ancient teachings are not relics of the past but living wisdom that continues to inspire, guide, and challenge us. By decoding the symbols that surround us and understanding the language of the cosmos, we open ourselves to a greater awareness of our place in the universe and the profound mysteries that lie within and beyond.

"To know the language of symbols is to hold the key to the universe, for it is through these sacred forms that the divine speaks to us."
Dr. Helena Armitage

Reflection Questions:

How do symbols and sacred geometry influence our perception of the world, and what deeper truths might they reveal about the nature of reality?

In what ways can understanding esoteric knowledge and sacred geometry enhance our spiritual growth and connection to the cosmos?

How can we incorporate the principles of sacred geometry and esoteric symbols into modern life, art, and architecture to create a more harmonious and meaningful existence?

PERSONAL REFLECTIONS AND TESTIMONIES

Awakening Through Symbols: A Seeker's Journey into Sacred Geometry

By Isabella Hartman

From a young age, I felt drawn to patterns and symbols that seemed to resonate with something deep within me. I would spend hours sketching intricate designs, unaware that these shapes held profound meanings rooted in ancient wisdom. My journey into esoteric knowledge truly began when I stumbled upon the concept of sacred geometry during a college art class.

The first symbol that captivated me was the Flower of Life. Its overlapping circles forming a perfectly symmetrical flower pattern seemed to hold a secret language. I learned that this symbol, found in temples and sacred sites around the world, was believed to contain the patterns of creation. This discovery ignited a thirst for understanding the connections between geometry, nature, and the cosmos.

I began to study the Platonic Solids, the Golden Ratio, and the Vesica Piscis. As I delved deeper, I realized that these geometric principles were not just mathematical concepts but representations of universal truths. They appeared in the spirals of galaxies, the petals of flowers, and even the proportions of the human body.

One profound experience was visiting Chartres Cathedral in France. Walking the labyrinth embedded in the floor, I felt a connection to the countless others who had walked the same path seeking spiritual enlightenment. The cathedral's architecture, infused with sacred geometry, seemed to vibrate with a higher energy. It was as if the building itself was a living testament to the harmony between humanity and the divine.

These experiences transformed my perception of the world. I began to see the interconnectedness of all things and understood that symbols and geometry are a universal language bridging the physical and spiritual realms. This realization led me to incorporate sacred geometry into my artwork and daily life, fostering a deeper sense of purpose and alignment with the universe.

The Alchemist Within: Embracing Personal Transformation

By Marcus Nguyen

My life took an unexpected turn when I encountered a personal crisis that left me searching for meaning. I felt lost, disconnected, and yearned for something that could help me make sense of my experiences. A friend introduced me to the concept of alchemy not the literal transformation of base metals into gold, but the metaphorical process of personal transformation and spiritual growth.

I immersed myself in studying alchemical texts, symbols like the Ouroboros, and the teachings of hermetic philosophy. The phrase "As above, so below; as within, so without" became a mantra that guided my introspection. I began to see that the outer chaos in my life was a reflection of inner turmoil.

Through meditation and journaling, I embarked on an inner alchemical journey. I confronted aspects of myself that I had long ignored fears, insecurities, and limiting beliefs. The process was challenging but profoundly healing. I visualized the transformation of these base aspects into higher virtues, much like the alchemists' pursuit of transmuting lead into gold.

One pivotal moment was during a meditation on the Phoenix, a symbol of rebirth and renewal. I imagined myself shedding old layers, allowing a new, empowered version of myself to emerge from the ashes of past experiences. This visualization brought a sense of liberation and hope.

Embracing the principles of alchemy taught me that transformation is an ongoing process. It requires patience, self-compassion, and a willingness to face the shadows within. This journey not only healed my relationship with myself but also improved my connections with others. I now view challenges as opportunities for growth and continue to apply alchemical principles to navigate life's complexities.

The Language of Light: Discovering the Power of Symbols in Healing

By Dr. Leila Ahmed

As a physician, I was trained to rely on empirical evidence and scientific methods. However, I always sensed that there was more to healing than what could be measured in a laboratory. My perspective shifted dramatically when I began exploring the role of symbols and sacred geometry in holistic healing.

I attended a workshop on energy medicine where I was introduced to the concept of the Merkaba a geometric symbol representing a vehicle of light and ascension. Intrigued, I started incorporating visualizations of the Merkaba and other sacred symbols into my meditation practice.

I noticed significant changes not only in my own well-being but also in how I connected with my patients. I began to see them as whole beings, with physical, emotional, and spiritual dimensions intricately linked. This holistic approach enhanced the effectiveness of treatments and fostered deeper trust and rapport.

Inspired, I pursued training in modalities like Reiki and sound healing, which often utilize symbols and vibrational frequencies. One memorable experience involved using the Flower of Life symbol during a healing session. A patient struggling with chronic pain reported a profound sense of peace and a noticeable reduction in symptoms afterward.

These experiences reinforced my belief that symbols and sacred geometry are powerful tools in healing. They serve as bridges between the conscious and subconscious mind, facilitating transformation and alignment with higher states of consciousness. Integrating esoteric knowledge into my medical practice has enriched my understanding of health and empowered my patients on their healing journeys.

PRACTICAL APPLICATIONS AND ACTION STEPS

Integrating Esoteric Knowledge into Everyday Life

Esoteric knowledge offers profound insights into the nature of reality, consciousness, and personal growth. By embracing these teachings, individuals can enhance their spiritual development and contribute to a more harmonious world. Here are practical steps to apply esoteric principles in daily life:

Study and Reflect on Sacred Symbols

- **Start with Basics**: Familiarize yourself with common esoteric symbols like the Ankh, Yin-Yang, and the Tree of Life. Understand their historical context and meanings.

- **Personal Connection**: Choose a symbol that resonates with you. Meditate on it, draw it, or incorporate it into your personal space to deepen your connection.

- **Symbol Journaling**: Keep a journal to record insights, dreams, or synchronicities related to symbols. Reflect on how they manifest in your life.

Explore Sacred Geometry

- **Visual Learning**: Watch documentaries or read books about sacred geometry to grasp concepts like the Golden Ratio and the Fibonacci sequence.

- **Creative Expression**: Engage in activities like drawing mandalas or constructing models of Platonic solids to internalize geometric principles.

- **Nature Observation**: Spend time in nature observing patterns spirals in shells, branching in trees, or the symmetry of flowers. Recognize the universal geometry at play.

Practice Meditation and Mindfulness

- **Symbol Meditation**: Focus your meditation on a specific symbol or geometric shape. Visualize it and contemplate its significance.

- **Breath Awareness**: Use breathing techniques to center yourself, enhancing your receptivity to esoteric insights.

- **Mindful Living**: Incorporate mindfulness into everyday activities, fostering a deeper awareness of the present moment and the interconnectedness of all things.

Engage in Energy Work

- **Learn Modalities**: Explore practices like Reiki, Qi Gong, or Tai Chi that involve working with subtle energies.

- **Chakra Balancing**: Study the chakra system and practice techniques to balance and align your energy centers.

- **Sound Healing**: Experiment with sound therapy using instruments like singing bowls or tuning forks, understanding the vibrational nature of the universe.

Study Esoteric Traditions and Philosophies

- **Read Foundational Texts**: Delve into works like the Emerald Tablet, The Kybalion, or texts on Kabbalah and Hermeticism.

- **Attend Lectures and Workshops**: Participate in events hosted by esoteric schools or spiritual centers to gain deeper insights.

- **Join Study Groups**: Connect with others who share an interest in esoteric studies to discuss ideas and experiences.

Incorporate Rituals and Ceremonies

- **Create Personal Rituals**: Design rituals that honor significant times like solstices, equinoxes, or lunar phases, aligning yourself with natural cycles.

- **Use Sacred Tools**: Incorporate items like crystals, incense, or tarot cards into your practices to enhance focus and intention.

- **Affirmations and Intentions**: Regularly set intentions and use affirmations to manifest desired outcomes, understanding the power of thought and word.

Cultivate Inner Alchemy

- **Self-Reflection**: Engage in practices that promote self-awareness, such as journaling or shadow work, to transform limiting beliefs and patterns.

- **Emotional Transmutation**: Learn techniques to transmute negative emotions into positive energy, drawing from alchemical principles.

- **Balance Dualities**: Embrace and integrate opposing aspects within yourself, achieving harmony and wholeness.

Connect with the Natural World

- **Ecotherapy**: Spend time in natural settings to ground yourself and attune to the Earth's energies.

- **Elemental Awareness**: Work with the elements earth, water, air, fire, and ether in meditation and ritual to deepen your connection to the physical and spiritual realms.

- **Gardening and Plant Wisdom**: Engage with plants, recognizing their healing properties and the wisdom they embody.

Develop Intuition and Psychic Abilities

- **Intuitive Practices**: Practice exercises that enhance intuition, such as card reading, scrying, or pendulum use.

- **Dream Work**: Keep a dream journal to explore messages from the subconscious mind and higher consciousness.

- **Psychic Development Classes**: Enroll in courses that focus on developing abilities like clairvoyance, clairaudience, or empathic skills.

Live Ethically and Compassionately

- **Universal Laws**: Study principles like the Law of Attraction, Law of Vibration, and Law of Cause and Effect, applying them to daily life.

- **Service to Others**: Volunteer and engage in acts of kindness, recognizing the interconnectedness of all beings.

- **Environmental Stewardship**: Adopt sustainable practices, honoring the Earth as a living entity deserving of respect and care.

Reflection Exercise

Contemplate how esoteric knowledge can influence your life:

- **What aspects of esoteric teachings resonate most with you, and why?**

- **How can you integrate esoteric practices into your daily routine to enhance your well-being?**

- **In what ways can you share esoteric wisdom to contribute to the collective consciousness and global harmony?**

Call to Action

Embracing esoteric knowledge is a personal journey of discovery and transformation. Begin by taking small steps choose a practice that speaks to you and commit to exploring it further. Seek out communities, mentors, and resources that support your growth.

Remember, the quest for understanding is lifelong. Be patient with yourself, stay open-minded, and trust the process. As you delve deeper into the mysteries, you'll find that the answers you seek often lead to even more profound questions, enriching your journey.

Final Thoughts

Esoteric knowledge bridges the gap between the seen and unseen, the known and the mysterious. It invites us to explore the depths of our inner selves and the vastness of the universe. By integrating these ancient teachings into our modern lives, we can foster a deeper connection to ourselves, each other, and the cosmos.

May your path be illuminated with wisdom, and may you find joy and fulfillment in the exploration of the sacred mysteries that surround us all.

PART V: QUANTUM MYSTERIES

CHAPTER 12: QUANTUM MYSTERIES BRIDGING THE GAP BETWEEN SCIENCE AND SPIRITUALITY, AND EXPLORING HOW CONSCIOUSNESS SHAPES REALITY

"We are not mere observers of the universe; we are active participants in its unfolding. Consciousness is not separate from reality but is a fundamental component of it a force that shapes the cosmos as much as it is shaped by it."

Dr. Caroline Sinclair

Prologue

The world of quantum physics is a realm of paradoxes, probabilities, and profound mysteries that challenge our understanding of reality. At its core, quantum mechanics suggests that the universe is not as solid or deterministic as classical physics once led us to believe. Instead, it is a dynamic, interconnected web where particles can exist in multiple states simultaneously, be influenced by observation, and even communicate instantaneously across vast distances. These discoveries have not only revolutionized science but have also sparked a profound dialogue between physics and spirituality, revealing that the boundaries between the material and the metaphysical are far more fluid than previously thought. Dr. Caroline Sinclair, a physicist and philosopher, guides us through the quantum mysteries that bridge science and spirituality, exploring how consciousness, intention, and the fabric of the universe are deeply intertwined.

Quantum Physics: The Science of the Unseen

Quantum physics, often described as the most successful theory in the history of science, delves into the fundamental nature of reality at the smallest scales. It reveals a world where particles behave in ways that defy classical logic, suggesting that the underlying structure of the universe is far stranger and more complex than we can perceive with our senses.

The Quantum World: A Realm of Paradoxes

- **Wave-Particle Duality: The Light That Is Both Particle and Wave**
  One of the most famous phenomena in quantum mechanics is wave-particle duality, which reveals that particles such as electrons and photons can exhibit both wave-like and particle-like properties depending on how

they are observed. In the famous double-slit experiment, particles behave like waves when unobserved, creating interference patterns on a screen. However, when a measurement is taken, these particles behave like discrete particles, as if they "know" they are being watched. This phenomenon suggests that observation itself plays a crucial role in determining the state of reality.

- **Quantum Superposition: Existing in Multiple States Simultaneously**
Superposition is the quantum principle that a particle can exist in multiple states at the same time until it is observed. A famous thought experiment illustrating this is Schrödinger's cat, where a cat in a sealed box is simultaneously alive and dead until the box is opened and observed. This concept challenges our understanding of reality as something fixed and objective, implying instead that it is fluid and dependent on observation.

- **Quantum Entanglement: The Spooky Action at a Distance**
Quantum entanglement occurs when particles become linked in such a way that the state of one particle instantly influences the state of another, no matter how far apart they are. Albert Einstein famously referred to this as "spooky action at a distance," as it seemed to violate the principles of locality and the speed of light. Entanglement suggests a deep, non-local connection between particles, hinting at an underlying oneness that transcends space and time.

The Observer Effect: Consciousness as a Co-Creator of Reality

- **The Role of the Observer in Quantum Mechanics**
One of the most profound implications of quantum physics is the role of the observer in shaping reality. Experiments suggest that the act of measurement collapses a particle's wave function, determining its

position or state. This raises fundamental questions about the nature of consciousness and its influence on the physical world. If observation can alter the outcome of quantum events, then reality itself may be influenced by conscious awareness.

- **The Copenhagen Interpretation: Reality Is Probabilistic, Not Deterministic**
The Copenhagen Interpretation, one of the most widely accepted interpretations of quantum mechanics, posits that particles exist in a state of probability until observed. Reality is not a fixed sequence of events but a series of potentialities that become actualized through observation. This interpretation aligns closely with certain spiritual teachings, which suggest that consciousness plays a direct role in the manifestation of reality.

- **The Participatory Universe: A Concept of Co-Creation**
Physicist John Wheeler proposed the idea of a "participatory universe," where observers are not passive witnesses to reality but active participants in its creation. According to Wheeler, the universe is fundamentally interactive, and our observations help bring it into being. This concept suggests that we are not separate from the cosmos but are intrinsically linked to its unfolding, with our consciousness acting as a co-creator of the physical world.

Quantum Field Theory: The Fabric of Reality

- **The Quantum Field: The Ground of All Being**
Quantum field theory expands the idea of particles to fields that permeate all of space. Particles are seen as excitations or "ripples" in these underlying fields, suggesting that the true nature of reality is not a collection of isolated objects but a unified field of energy and information. This concept resonates with spiritual

traditions that describe the universe as a singular, interconnected whole, often referred to as the "quantum vacuum" or the "field of potential."

- **Zero-Point Energy: The Energy of the Vacuum**
Zero-point energy refers to the lowest possible energy state of a quantum system, even at absolute zero temperature. This "vacuum energy" is not empty but teems with virtual particles that pop in and out of existence, suggesting that the very fabric of space is alive with energy. Some theorists propose that zero-point energy could be harnessed as a limitless power source, and esoteric traditions view it as the creative force of the cosmos the source from which all matter and consciousness emerge.

- **Quantum Foam and the Fabric of Spacetime**
At the smallest scales, spacetime itself is thought to be a seething, frothy sea known as quantum foam. This concept challenges our understanding of the universe as a smooth, continuous expanse, revealing instead a dynamic, ever-changing fabric where space and time are constantly fluctuating. The implications of quantum foam suggest that the universe is fundamentally uncertain and that reality is far more fluid and interconnected than we can perceive.

The Bridge Between Science and Spirituality: Consciousness, Intention, and the Nature of Reality

The revelations of quantum physics are not just scientific; they have profound implications for spirituality and the nature of consciousness. For centuries, spiritual traditions have taught that reality is shaped by the mind, that all things are connected, and that we are active participants in the cosmos. Quantum physics provides a scientific framework that aligns with these ancient teachings, suggesting that the boundaries between science and spirituality are not as rigid as once thought.

Consciousness as a Fundamental Force

- **The Primacy of Consciousness Hypothesis**
  Some physicists and philosophers argue that consciousness is not a byproduct of the brain but a fundamental aspect of reality, as essential as space, time, and matter. This view, known as the primacy of consciousness, suggests that the mind is not confined to the physical body but is part of a larger, universal consciousness that permeates the cosmos. This idea aligns with spiritual teachings that describe the universe as a manifestation of divine consciousness or a "mind of God."

- **Panpsychism: Consciousness in All Things**
  Panpsychism is the philosophical belief that consciousness is a fundamental property of all matter, not just humans and animals. According to this view, even the smallest particles possess a form of awareness, contributing to a collective, universal mind. Panpsychism offers a bridge between quantum physics and spirituality, suggesting that the entire universe is alive, conscious, and interconnected.

- **The Hard Problem of Consciousness and Quantum Solutions**
  The "hard problem" of consciousness, as defined by philosopher David Chalmers, refers to the challenge of explaining how subjective experience arises from physical processes. Quantum theories of consciousness propose that the brain may operate at the quantum level, allowing it to interact with the quantum field in ways that conventional neuroscience cannot explain. These theories suggest that consciousness is deeply embedded in the fabric of reality and that understanding it requires

a new, holistic approach that integrates both science and spirituality.

The Power of Intention: Mind Over Matter

- ### The Placebo Effect: Mind as Healer
  The placebo effect, where patients experience real improvements in health after receiving a treatment with no active ingredients, demonstrates the power of belief and intention. This phenomenon suggests that the mind can influence the body's healing processes in ways that are not yet fully understood by conventional science. The placebo effect aligns with quantum theories that posit consciousness as a force that can affect physical reality.

- ### Intentional Healing: Quantum Touch and Energy Medicine
  Energy healing modalities such as Reiki, Quantum Touch, and Pranic Healing operate on the principle that intention and focused awareness can direct energy to promote healing. Practitioners of these modalities believe that by channeling energy through the hands, they can influence the body's energy field, harmonizing it and restoring balance. Quantum physics provides a possible explanation for these practices, suggesting that the healer's consciousness interacts with the patient's quantum field, facilitating changes at the subatomic level.

- ### The Global Consciousness Project: Coherent Intention and Collective Reality
  The Global Consciousness Project, led by researchers at Princeton University, monitors random number generators around the world to detect shifts in global consciousness. Studies have found that during major world events such as natural disasters, global meditations, or significant cultural moments the randomness of these devices decreases, suggesting that collective human intention can influence physical

systems. These findings support the idea that consciousness is not isolated but has a measurable impact on the world around us.

Non-Local Consciousness: Beyond Space and Time

- **Remote Viewing and the Non-Local Mind**
Remote viewing is a practice where individuals attempt to perceive information about a distant or unseen target, often under controlled conditions. Research by government agencies, including the CIA's Stargate Project, has demonstrated that trained individuals can access information beyond their immediate sensory reach, suggesting that consciousness is not confined by space or time. These findings support the idea of a non-local mind that can connect with the quantum field, accessing information through means that defy classical explanations.

- **Out-of-Body Experiences (OBEs) and Near-Death Experiences (NDEs)**
Out-of-body and near-death experiences provide anecdotal evidence that consciousness can exist independently of the physical body. During NDEs, individuals often report heightened awareness, encounters with light beings, and vivid experiences of realms beyond our physical reality. Some accounts include accurate observations of events occurring while the person was clinically unconscious, challenging conventional neuroscience and supporting theories of consciousness as a non-local phenomenon.

- **Quantum Consciousness and the Holographic Universe**
The holographic principle suggests that the universe can be thought of as a vast, interconnected hologram, where every part contains information about the whole. This idea, supported by some interpretations of black

hole physics, implies that reality is fundamentally interconnected and that consciousness plays a vital role in the structure of the cosmos. In a holographic universe, each individual's consciousness is a reflection of the larger, universal mind, with every thought and action resonating throughout the entire field.

The Quantum Connection: Spiritual Traditions and Modern Physics

The parallels between quantum physics and spiritual traditions are striking, suggesting that ancient wisdom and modern science are two sides of the same coin. Many spiritual teachings, from Eastern mysticism to Indigenous worldviews, resonate with the principles uncovered by quantum mechanics, offering a deeper understanding of how consciousness and reality are interwoven.

The Tao of Physics: Parallels with Eastern Mysticism

- **Buddhism and the Illusion of Separation**
  Buddhism teaches that the self is an illusion, a transient assembly of thoughts, emotions, and sensations that arise and dissipate within a larger field of awareness. This view aligns with quantum physics, which suggests that individuality is an emergent phenomenon rather than an inherent property of matter. The interconnectedness highlighted by entanglement mirrors the Buddhist concept of *interbeing* the idea that all things are connected and that nothing exists in isolation.

- **The Tao and the Flow of the Quantum Field**
  The Tao, as described in Taoism, is the ultimate source and flow of existence, a dynamic and formless reality that gives rise to all things. The Tao's emphasis on the balance of opposites, fluidity, and the underlying unity of the cosmos closely mirrors the principles of quantum field theory, where particles are seen as

transient manifestations of a deeper, unified field. Taoist philosophy's focus on harmony with the natural order resonates with quantum physics 'vision of a non-dualistic universe.

- **Hinduism and the Dance of Shiva**
  In Hindu mythology, Shiva's cosmic dance symbolizes the creation, preservation, and dissolution of the universe, reflecting the dynamic, ever-changing nature of reality. This metaphor aligns with the quantum view of the universe as a ceaseless flow of energy and transformation, where particles continually emerge, interact, and dissolve back into the field. The cyclical dance of Shiva echoes the quantum dance of particles, matter, and energy, revealing a universe that is constantly in motion.

Indigenous Wisdom and Quantum Reality

- **Native American Teachings on the Web of Life**
  Indigenous cultures around the world have long held the view that all life is interconnected, that the earth, sky, and living beings are bound together in a web of relationships. This perspective parallels the quantum concept of entanglement, where the actions of one particle affect others instantaneously, regardless of distance. Indigenous teachings emphasize respect, reciprocity, and a deep connection with the natural world, reflecting a quantum understanding of reality as a seamless whole.

- **Shamanism and Non-Ordinary Reality**
  Shamanic traditions teach that the physical world is only one aspect of a multi-layered reality that includes spirit realms, ancestral wisdom, and energies that transcend the material plane. Shamans, through altered states of consciousness, access these non-ordinary realities to heal, gain insight, and communicate with higher intelligences. Quantum physics, with its exploration of dimensions beyond our perception, supports the idea that our

everyday reality is just one slice of a much broader and more mysterious existence.

- ### Dreamtime and the Quantum Dream
  In Aboriginal Australian cosmology, Dreamtime represents a time outside of time, a parallel reality where the spiritual and material worlds converge. It is a realm where ancestors, spirits, and living beings coexist, and where the laws of the physical world do not apply. The concept of Dreamtime resonates with quantum theories that suggest time is not linear and that all moments coexist simultaneously within a timeless field. This view aligns with the idea that consciousness can transcend the bounds of space and time, accessing deeper truths about existence.

The Science of Meditation: Altering Consciousness and Reality

- ### The Quantum Mind and Meditative States
  Meditation is known to alter brain activity, promote healing, and enhance cognitive functions, but it may also provide a window into the quantum nature of consciousness. Studies have shown that deep meditative states can synchronize brain waves, induce coherence in the heart's electromagnetic field, and even alter genetic expression. These effects suggest that meditation not only changes the individual but also interacts with the quantum field, influencing reality at a fundamental level.

- ### The Power of Collective Meditation and Global Impact
  Research on collective meditation has demonstrated that large groups meditating together can reduce crime rates, lower stress in surrounding populations, and promote peace in conflict zones. Known as the Maharishi Effect, this phenomenon indicates that focused, coherent intention can create measurable changes in the external world, supporting the quantum hypothesis that

consciousness is interconnected and capable of affecting reality on a grand scale.

- **Kundalini Awakening and Quantum Activation**
  Kundalini, often described as a coiled serpent of energy at the base of the spine, represents the awakening of spiritual potential and the connection to higher consciousness. When activated, Kundalini energy rises through the body's energy centers, leading to profound physical, mental, and spiritual transformations. This process can be likened to a quantum activation, where dormant potentials within the individual are unlocked, aligning them with the cosmic flow of energy and information.

Implications of Quantum Mysteries: A New Paradigm for Humanity

The exploration of quantum mysteries reveals that our understanding of reality is far from complete and that consciousness plays a far more significant role than previously acknowledged. These insights are not just theoretical; they have practical implications for how we live, perceive, and interact with the world.

Shifting Worldviews: From Mechanistic to Holistic

- **A New Science of Interconnectedness**
  The shift from a mechanistic worldview, where the universe is seen as a clockwork machine of separate parts, to a holistic paradigm that recognizes interconnectedness, offers profound implications for science, medicine, and society. This new science emphasizes the importance of relationships, systems, and the flow of information, encouraging approaches that honor the complexity and interdependence of all things.

- **Healing and Holistic Medicine**

The recognition of consciousness as a fundamental force invites a new approach to healing that integrates mind, body, and spirit. Holistic medicine, energy healing, and complementary therapies align with quantum principles, viewing illness not just as a physical imbalance but as a disruption in the flow of consciousness and energy. Healing becomes a process of restoring harmony, coherence, and alignment with the deeper patterns of the universe.

- **Technology in Harmony with Nature**
As our understanding of quantum mechanics grows, so too does our ability to develop technologies that work in harmony with natural systems. Quantum computing, zero-point energy, and biomimetic designs inspired by nature's geometry represent the next frontier of innovation one that honors the balance of the quantum world and its interconnected web of life.

Consciousness and the Future of Human Potential

- **The Expansion of Human Abilities**
If consciousness is indeed a fundamental aspect of reality, then the limits of human potential are far greater than we currently understand. Psychic phenomena, telepathy, remote viewing, and other abilities that have long been relegated to the realm of the paranormal may be seen as natural extensions of the quantum mind. The future may hold the development of new practices, technologies, and educational models that cultivate these latent potentials, expanding the boundaries of what it means to be human.

- **Creating Reality Through Intention**
Quantum physics suggests that we are not passive observers but active participants in the creation of our reality. This understanding empowers us to take responsibility for our thoughts, beliefs, and actions, recognizing that our intentions shape the world around

us. By cultivating positive, coherent, and compassionate intentions, we can collectively manifest a more harmonious and enlightened reality.

- **The Evolution of Consciousness and Global Awakening** As more people explore the intersection of quantum science and spirituality, there is a growing sense of global awakening a shift toward higher consciousness that transcends individual, cultural, and national boundaries. This evolution of consciousness invites us to see ourselves as interconnected beings, part of a larger cosmic story that is unfolding in real-time. Embracing this new understanding can inspire a renaissance of creativity, empathy, and innovation that has the power to transform our world.

Conclusion

Quantum mysteries challenge us to rethink everything we know about reality, consciousness, and the nature of existence. They offer a bridge between the material and the spiritual, between science and ancient wisdom, revealing that the universe is not a static, deterministic machine but a living, dynamic field of infinite possibilities. As we continue to explore the quantum realm, we are reminded that the most profound discoveries lie not just in the outer world but within ourselves.

The journey into quantum mysteries is not merely an intellectual pursuit; it is a call to awaken to our own potential as co-creators of reality. By embracing the interconnectedness of all things and recognizing the power of consciousness, we can navigate the complexities of the modern world with a renewed sense of wonder, purpose, and responsibility.

"The true mystery of the universe is not in the stars above, but in the consciousness that seeks to understand them. We are not separate from the cosmos we are the cosmos, aware of itself."
Dr. Caroline Sinclair

Reflection Questions:

How does the relationship between consciousness and reality challenge traditional scientific and philosophical views of the universe?

In what ways can the insights of quantum physics inspire new approaches to healing, technology, and human potential?

What practical steps can individuals take to align their consciousness with the principles of quantum mechanics and actively participate in shaping their own reality?

PERSONAL REFLECTIONS AND TESTIMONIES

Beyond the Veil: A Physicist's Exploration of Consciousness

By Dr. Elizabeth Carter

As a quantum physicist, I dedicated years to understanding the fundamental nature of reality. My work revolved around particles, waves, and the mathematical equations that govern their behavior. Yet, despite the elegance of quantum mechanics, I couldn't shake the feeling that something profound was missing a deeper understanding of how consciousness fits into the grand tapestry of the universe.

The turning point came during a research sabbatical in Switzerland, where I collaborated with a team studying quantum entanglement. We observed particles instantaneously affecting each other over vast distances, defying classical notions of space and time. This phenomenon, known as "spooky action at a distance," left me both exhilarated and perplexed. How could particles be so intimately connected, regardless of the space between them?

One evening, while reflecting on these mysteries, I encountered the works of physicist David Bohm and his concept of the "Implicate Order." Bohm proposed that at a fundamental level, the universe is an undivided whole, with all parts interconnected in ways that transcend our conventional understanding of reality. This idea resonated deeply with me, igniting a curiosity about the relationship between consciousness and the quantum world.

I began exploring interdisciplinary studies, delving into philosophy, neuroscience, and Eastern mysticism. I was particularly drawn to the parallels between quantum mechanics and the teachings of Vedanta and Buddhism, which speak of a unified consciousness underlying all existence.

During a meditation retreat, I experienced a profound shift in awareness. As I focused inward, I felt a dissolution of boundaries a sense of unity with everything around me. It was as if I had tapped into the very fabric of reality that quantum physics hinted at but couldn't fully explain. This personal encounter with consciousness as a fundamental aspect of the universe transformed my perspective.

Returning to my research with renewed purpose, I began investigating the role of the observer in quantum experiments. The famous double-slit experiment demonstrates that particles behave differently when observed, suggesting that consciousness influences physical reality. While controversial, this line of inquiry opened up new possibilities for understanding the interplay between mind and matter.

My journey has led me to advocate for a more holistic approach to science one that embraces the mysteries of consciousness rather than dismissing them. I believe that by integrating subjective experience with objective investigation, we can unlock deeper truths about the universe and our place within it.

The Healer's Insight: Quantum Biology and the Power of Intention

By Dr. Anjali Singh

As a medical doctor specializing in oncology, I witnessed the devastating impact of cancer on patients and their families. Despite advances in treatment, I often felt that something was missing in our approach to healing. My interest in alternative therapies led me to explore the emerging field of quantum biology a discipline examining the quantum phenomena occurring within living organisms.

I was fascinated by studies suggesting that processes like photosynthesis, bird navigation, and even our sense of smell might involve quantum mechanics. If quantum effects play a role in biological systems, could they also influence human health and healing?

My curiosity deepened when I encountered research on the placebo effect and spontaneous remissions. Patients sometimes experienced remarkable recoveries that couldn't be fully explained by medical interventions alone. I began to wonder whether consciousness and intention could directly impact the body's healing processes at a quantum level.

To explore this possibility, I incorporated mindfulness practices and guided imagery into my patient care. I encouraged patients to visualize their immune systems attacking cancer cells, fostering a positive and proactive mindset. The results were encouraging patients reported reduced anxiety, improved well-being, and in some cases, better treatment outcomes.

One patient, Sarah, left a lasting impression on me. Diagnosed with stage IV cancer, her prognosis was grim. Together, we integrated conventional therapy with meditation and intentional healing practices. Sarah visualized her body healing and embraced a holistic lifestyle. Over time, her scans showed significant tumor reduction, defying expectations.

These experiences led me to collaborate with researchers studying the effects of consciousness on physical matter.

Experiments involving random number generators and water crystallization suggested that focused intention could influence outcomes in subtle but measurable ways. While the mechanisms remain elusive, the implications are profound.

I now advocate for a paradigm shift in medicine one that recognizes the role of consciousness in health. By embracing the quantum mysteries of life, we can develop more compassionate, effective approaches to healing that honor the mind-body connection.

Entangled Minds: A Psychologist's Encounter with Quantum Consciousness

By Dr. Michael Bennett

As a clinical psychologist, I spent years helping individuals navigate the complexities of the human mind. My practice was grounded in evidence-based therapies, yet I occasionally encountered phenomena that challenged conventional explanations patients sharing telepathic experiences, precognitive dreams, or a deep sense of interconnectedness with others.

Skeptical but intrigued, I began researching the intersections between psychology and quantum physics. I discovered the work of Dean Radin and the field of parapsychology, which scientifically investigates psychic phenomena. Studies on telepathy, remote viewing, and psychokinesis suggested that consciousness might extend beyond the confines of the brain.

One experiment that captivated me involved pairs of participants separated by distance. When one person was exposed to stimuli causing emotional responses, the other exhibited corresponding brainwave patterns, despite no sensory communication. This "entanglement" of minds hinted at a quantum connection between consciousnesses.

Inspired, I incorporated mindfulness and meditation techniques into my therapy sessions, aiming to tap into this deeper level of awareness. Patients reported heightened intuition, enhanced empathy, and a greater sense of connection with others.

A personal experience solidified my belief in quantum consciousness. While meditating, I had a vivid impression of an old friend I hadn't spoken to in years. Compelled to reach out, I discovered that he was going through a difficult time and had been thinking of me. The synchronicity was striking, suggesting that our minds were linked in ways beyond physical interaction.

These experiences led me to theorize that consciousness operates on a quantum level, transcending space and time. By acknowledging and exploring these connections, we can foster greater understanding, healing, and unity in both individual and collective contexts.

PRACTICAL APPLICATIONS AND ACTION STEPS

Bridging Science and Spirituality: Harnessing Quantum Mysteries in Daily Life

The quantum realm offers fascinating insights into the nature of reality and consciousness. By exploring and applying these principles, individuals can deepen their understanding of themselves and the universe. Here are practical steps to integrate quantum concepts into everyday life:

Cultivate Mindfulness and Presence

- **Meditation Practices**: Engage in regular meditation to quiet the mind and become more attuned to subtle aspects of consciousness. Techniques like mindfulness, transcendental meditation, or loving-kindness can enhance awareness.

- **Mindful Observation**: Practice being fully present in daily activities. Pay attention to sensations, thoughts, and emotions without judgment, fostering a deeper connection to the present moment.

- **Breath Awareness**: Focus on your breath as an anchor to the here and now. This practice can help you become more sensitive to shifts in consciousness and energy.

Explore the Mind-Matter Connection

- **Intention Setting**: Begin each day by setting clear, positive intentions. Recognize that your thoughts and intentions may influence your experiences and interactions.

- **Visualization Techniques**: Use guided imagery to envision desired outcomes, whether for personal goals, healing, or enhancing relationships.

- **Gratitude Practice**: Cultivate an attitude of gratitude to raise your vibrational frequency, aligning yourself with positive energy.

Study Quantum Concepts

- **Educational Resources**: Read books and watch documentaries on quantum physics and consciousness. Works by authors like Dr. Amit Goswami, Dr. Fred Alan Wolf, and Dr. Bruce Lipton offer accessible insights.

- **Online Courses**: Enroll in courses or workshops that delve into quantum mechanics, neurobiology, and their implications for consciousness.

- **Discussion Groups**: Join or form study groups to discuss and explore quantum concepts with others who share your interest.

Embrace Interconnectedness

- **Community Engagement**: Participate in community activities that promote unity and cooperation, reflecting the interconnected nature of reality.

- **Environmental Stewardship**: Recognize your connection to the Earth by adopting sustainable practices and advocating for ecological preservation.

- **Empathy Development**: Practice active listening and

empathy in interactions, fostering deeper connections with others.

Experiment with Conscious Influence

- **Mindful Eating**: Pay attention to the energy and intention you bring to food preparation and consumption. Bless or express gratitude for your meals.

- **Energy Healing**: Explore modalities like Reiki, Qi Gong, or Healing Touch that work with subtle energy fields influenced by consciousness.

- **Conscious Technology Use**: Be mindful of your relationship with technology, using it intentionally rather than compulsively.

Foster Creativity and Innovation

- **Artistic Expression**: Engage in creative pursuits like painting, music, or writing to tap into the flow state where quantum insights may emerge.

- **Problem-Solving**: Apply quantum thinking by considering multiple possibilities and embracing uncertainty in decision-making processes.

- **Innovation Spaces**: Create environments that encourage open-minded exploration and collaboration, such as innovation labs or think tanks.

Practice Non-Local Awareness

- **Remote Connection Exercises**: Attempt to sense or connect with someone at a distance, focusing on shared thoughts or emotions.

- **Dream Journaling**: Keep a record of your dreams, noting any instances of precognition or shared experiences with others.

- **Synchronicity Awareness**: Pay attention to meaningful

coincidences and consider their potential significance in your life.

Integrate Mind-Body Practices

- **Yoga and Movement**: Incorporate practices that unite mind and body, enhancing awareness of the subtle energies within and around you.

- **Biofeedback and Neurofeedback**: Use technology to gain insight into physiological processes and learn to consciously influence them.

- **Holistic Health Approaches**: Embrace wellness practices that consider the whole person physical, mental, emotional, and spiritual.

Engage in Collective Consciousness Activities

- **Group Meditation**: Participate in synchronized meditations or global events aimed at raising collective consciousness.

- **Community Service**: Volunteer for causes that align with higher principles, contributing to positive change in the world.

- **Peace Projects**: Support initiatives focused on conflict resolution, understanding that individual consciousness contributes to collective realities.

Reflect on Personal Beliefs and Perceptions

- **Question Assumptions**: Regularly examine your beliefs about reality, remaining open to new insights and perspectives.

- **Embrace Paradox**: Accept that some aspects of existence may be inherently paradoxical, allowing for a more flexible understanding of the world.

- **Cultivate Humility**: Recognize the limits of current

knowledge and maintain a sense of wonder about the mysteries yet to be uncovered.

Reflection Exercise

Consider how quantum mysteries resonate with your personal experiences:

• **What aspects of quantum concepts intrigue you the most, and why?**

• **How can exploring the relationship between consciousness and reality enhance your understanding of yourself and the world?**

• **In what ways can you apply quantum principles to foster personal growth and contribute positively to others?**

Call to Action

Embracing quantum mysteries invites us to expand our consciousness and explore the interconnected fabric of reality. Begin by integrating small practices into your daily routine meditate, set intentions, or engage in mindful observation. Seek out educational resources and communities that support your journey.

Remember, the quest to understand quantum mysteries is both a personal and collective endeavor. As we deepen our awareness, we contribute to a global shift towards greater unity, compassion, and understanding. Your exploration can inspire others, creating ripples of positive change throughout the fabric of existence.

Final Thoughts

Quantum mysteries challenge us to rethink our understanding of reality, inviting us to consider that consciousness and the universe are intricately linked. By exploring these concepts, we open ourselves to new possibilities and deeper connections with all that is.

May your journey into the quantum realm enrich your life, expand your horizons, and illuminate the boundless potential that resides within and around you.

PART VI: HUMAN POTENTIAL

CHAPTER 13: HUMAN POTENTIAL UNLOCKING THE LATENT ABILITIES WITHIN US, FROM PSYCHIC PHENOMENA TO COLLECTIVE CONSCIOUSNESS

"We are far more powerful and interconnected than we dare to imagine. To unlock the full potential of humanity, we must look beyond the limits of the physical and embrace the extraordinary capacities that lie within each of us."

Dr. Amelia Dawson

Prologue

The exploration of human potential is a journey into the unknown realms of the mind, body, and spirit. For centuries, mystics, sages, and visionaries have spoken of extraordinary human abilities telepathy, precognition, healing, and more that lie dormant within us all. These capabilities, often dismissed as fringe or paranormal, are now being revisited through the lens of modern science, psychology, and quantum theories of consciousness. Dr. Amelia Dawson, a pioneer in the study of human potential, takes us on a deep dive into the untapped abilities that reside within us, revealing how ancient wisdom, cutting-edge research, and collective awakening are converging to redefine what it means to be human. This chapter uncovers the latent powers within, exploring how unlocking these abilities could transform not only our individual lives but also our shared future.

The Latent Powers of the Human Mind: Exploring Psychic Phenomena

The human mind is capable of far more than conventional science has traditionally acknowledged. Psychic phenomena, once relegated to the realm of superstition, are increasingly being studied by researchers who are uncovering evidence that supports the existence of extraordinary mental abilities. These abilities suggest that consciousness extends beyond the brain, connecting us in ways that transcend the limitations of space and time.

Telepathy: The Mind-to-Mind Connection

- **The Science of Telepathy**
  Telepathy, or the direct transmission of thoughts between individuals, has been a subject of fascination across cultures and ages. Modern experiments have provided intriguing evidence of telepathic communication, especially between individuals with close emotional bonds. Studies using functional MRI and EEG have shown that when one person focuses on transmitting thoughts to another, corresponding brain wave patterns can be

observed in the recipient, even when they are separated by great distances. These findings suggest that telepathy may not be a mere fantasy but a latent ability rooted in the quantum interconnectedness of consciousness.

- **Remote Viewing and Military Applications**
  During the Cold War, both the United States and the Soviet Union conducted classified research into remote viewing an ability to perceive distant or unseen targets using extrasensory perception. Projects like the CIA's Stargate Program employed psychics to gather intelligence on enemy activities, sometimes with startling accuracy. Remote viewers described foreign facilities, events, and even hidden objects in detail, contributing to military strategies and decision-making. While these programs were eventually declassified, they highlight the potential of the human mind to access information beyond conventional means.

- **Telepathic Communication in Animals**
  Telepathy is not limited to humans; animals often display behaviors suggesting a form of mind-to-mind communication. Pet owners frequently report instances of their pets sensing their return home or knowing when they are ill. Studies on animal telepathy have observed phenomena such as synchronized behaviors in separated animals, suggesting a deep, non-verbal connection. The concept of morphic resonance, proposed by biologist Rupert Sheldrake, posits that species share a collective memory that enables such telepathic exchanges, further blurring the boundaries between individual minds.

Precognition: Seeing Beyond the Present Moment

- **Premonitions and Predictive Dreams**
  Precognition, the ability to perceive future events before they occur, often manifests in dreams, flashes of insight, or gut feelings. Documented cases include

individuals having detailed premonitions of natural disasters, accidents, or personal events that later come to pass. Researchers studying precognition have found statistical evidence suggesting that the mind can respond to stimuli a few seconds before they occur, as measured by physiological responses such as changes in heart rate or brain activity. These findings challenge our linear perception of time, suggesting that consciousness may have access to information from the future.

- **The Global Consciousness Project and Predictive Patterns**
The Global Consciousness Project's random number generators, which detect deviations during major global events, have occasionally shown patterns before these events unfold. These predictive anomalies suggest that consciousness may have a form of foresight, collectively sensing disturbances before they happen. This phenomenon implies a deeper, interconnected awareness that transcends individual minds, hinting at a collective precognitive ability embedded within humanity.

- **Synchronicity: Meaningful Coincidences as Clues to the Future**
Synchronicities, or meaningful coincidences that seem too significant to be random, often serve as indicators of precognitive insight. Carl Jung, who coined the term, believed that synchronicities arise from the alignment of external events with internal states of mind, reflecting a deeper, interconnected order. People frequently report experiencing synchronicities during times of heightened intuition, creativity, or spiritual awakening, suggesting that these moments may be windows into the non-linear nature of time and consciousness.

Psychokinesis: Mind Over Matter

- **The Power of the Mind to Influence Physical Objects**

Psychokinesis, or the ability to move or alter physical objects with the mind, has long been a staple of paranormal research. Experiments in controlled settings have shown small but statistically significant effects where participants influence random number generators, bend metal objects, or alter the behavior of living cells through focused intention. While often controversial, these studies suggest that the mind's influence extends beyond the body, capable of affecting the material world in ways that defy conventional physics.

- **The Placebo Effect as a Form of Psychokinesis**
  The placebo effect is often cited as an example of mind over matter, where belief and expectation trigger real physiological changes. Patients receiving placebos can experience reductions in pain, improvements in mood, and even measurable changes in brain chemistry simply because they believe they are receiving effective treatment. This phenomenon illustrates that consciousness can directly influence the body, blurring the line between mental intention and physical reality.

- **Tulpas and Thought-Forms: Manifestations of Focused Thought**
  In Tibetan Buddhism, Tulpas are thought-forms entities created purely through the power of concentrated thought and belief. Practitioners train to visualize these forms so vividly that they seem to take on a life of their own, influencing the environment or even interacting with others. The concept of Tulpas demonstrates that focused intention and mental imagery can manifest phenomena that appear tangible, reinforcing the idea that consciousness can shape reality in profound ways.

Collective Consciousness: The Power of Unity and Shared Intent

Beyond individual abilities, the concept of collective consciousness suggests that humanity shares a vast, interconnected mind that transcends individual experience. This collective field of awareness influences societies, cultures, and even global events, highlighting the power of unity and shared intent.

The Noosphere: A Global Mind

- **The Noosphere and the Evolution of Consciousness**
The term "Noosphere," coined by philosopher Pierre Teilhard de Chardin and scientist Vladimir Vernadsky, refers to the sphere of human thought that surrounds the Earth, much like the atmosphere. This concept envisions the collective consciousness of humanity as a living, evolving entity that influences and is influenced by our actions, thoughts, and intentions. As the Noosphere grows more interconnected through technology and shared experiences, it reflects the evolution of human consciousness toward a unified global mind.

- **The Hundredth Monkey Effect: A Metaphor for Collective Learning**
The Hundredth Monkey Effect describes a phenomenon in which a new behavior or knowledge spontaneously spreads across a population once a critical mass has been reached. Although the original account of the effect has been debated, the concept captures the essence of collective consciousness that when enough individuals adopt a new way of thinking or acting, it can ripple through the collective, influencing others in ways that seem instantaneous. This effect suggests that our minds are not isolated but are part of a larger, interconnected network.

- **Social Media and the Digital Consciousness**
The rise of social media has accelerated the emergence of a digital Noosphere, where thoughts, ideas, and emotions

spread rapidly across the globe. This digital consciousness has the power to unite people around causes, spark revolutions, or propagate misinformation. It reflects the double-edged nature of collective consciousness capable of profound creativity, empathy, and connection, but also susceptible to manipulation and division. The digital age offers both the opportunity and the challenge of harnessing collective intent for positive transformation.

Group Meditation and the Coherence Effect

- **The Maharishi Effect: Coherent Group Meditation and Societal Impact**
  The Maharishi Effect, named after Maharishi Mahesh Yogi, suggests that when a critical mass of individuals meditates together with a focus on peace and coherence, measurable changes occur in society, including reductions in crime, violence, and conflict. Studies have documented these effects during mass meditation events, indicating that the collective field generated by focused intention can influence the broader environment. This phenomenon underscores the power of collective consciousness to bring about positive change through shared effort.

- **Global Meditation Movements and Conscious Activism**
  In recent years, global meditation movements have emerged as a form of conscious activism, uniting people worldwide to meditate for peace, healing, and planetary well-being. Events like the Global Synchronized Meditation and the International Day of Peace draw millions of participants who focus their collective intention on creating a better world. These movements demonstrate the potential of collective consciousness to transcend borders, cultures, and differences, harnessing the power of unity for a common purpose.

- **Healing Circles and Community Intention**
  Healing circles, where individuals come together to focus their energy on a person in need, are a testament to the power of collective intention. Whether conducted in person or virtually, these circles often report significant improvements in the physical, emotional, and spiritual well-being of those receiving the group's focused attention. The success of such practices highlights the profound impact of collective consciousness, where the power of the group amplifies the healing potential of each individual.

The Emergence of a New Humanity

- **The Great Awakening: A Shift in Global Consciousness**
  Around the world, people are experiencing what has been described as a Great Awakening a shift in consciousness that transcends traditional boundaries of race, religion, and nationality. This awakening is characterized by a heightened awareness of interconnectedness, a longing for spiritual growth, and a rejection of materialism in favor of deeper values. As more individuals tap into their latent abilities and embrace the power of collective consciousness, humanity is poised to enter a new era of enlightenment and global unity.

- **Superhuman Abilities and the Next Evolutionary Leap**
  The idea that humanity is on the brink of an evolutionary leap is supported by the emergence of individuals exhibiting extraordinary abilities often referred to as "superhumans." These individuals display advanced cognitive, physical, and spiritual skills, from enhanced intuition and accelerated learning to spontaneous healing and altered states of consciousness. Their experiences suggest that what we consider paranormal today may be the norm for future generations, as humanity evolves to unlock its full potential.

- **Building a Future Guided by Conscious Evolution**
  Conscious evolution is the deliberate effort to shape our personal and collective development through mindfulness, intentional living, and a commitment to higher values. This concept empowers individuals and societies to take an active role in their own evolution, recognizing that our choices, thoughts, and actions contribute to the unfolding story of humanity. By embracing conscious evolution, we can create a future where human potential is fully realized, and the collective consciousness reflects the best of who we are.

Conclusion

The exploration of human potential reveals that we are far more than the sum of our physical parts. Our minds possess extraordinary abilities that connect us to each other and the cosmos in ways that defy conventional understanding. By unlocking these latent powers, embracing the interconnectedness of collective consciousness, and recognizing our role as co-creators of reality, we can transcend the limitations that have held us back.

This awakening to our true potential is not just a personal journey but a collective one one that calls us to rise above fear, division, and doubt, and to step into a new era of possibility. The hidden abilities within us are not just gifts but responsibilities, urging us to use our power wisely, compassionately, and for the greater good.

"The future of humanity lies not in the stars, but in the untapped potential within each of us. By awakening to who we truly are, we can shape a world that reflects the highest aspirations of our collective soul."
Dr. Amelia Dawson

Reflection Questions:

What latent abilities might you possess that have yet to be fully realized, and how can you begin to explore and develop them?

How can the power of collective consciousness be harnessed to address global challenges and create a more unified and compassionate world?

What role do you see for yourself in the ongoing evolution of human potential, and how can you contribute to the awakening of humanity?

PERSONAL REFLECTIONS AND TESTIMONIES

Awakening the Inner Vision: A Journey into Psychic Phenomena

By Sophia Reynolds

From a young age, I knew I was different. While other children played games, I found myself drawn to the unseen world. I would often have vivid dreams that later unfolded in reality small glimpses of conversations or events that hadn't yet occurred. My parents dismissed them as coincidences, but as I grew older, the experiences intensified.

In my teenage years, I began to sense the emotions of others deeply. Walking into a room, I could feel the lingering sadness, joy, or anxiety as if they were my own emotions. It was overwhelming, and without understanding what was happening, I felt isolated and confused.

It wasn't until I stumbled upon a book on psychic development that I realized I might possess empathic and precognitive abilities. Determined to understand and control these experiences, I sought out mentors and joined a community of like-minded individuals. Through meditation, energy work, and focused practice, I began to hone my abilities.

One of the most profound experiences occurred during a group meditation session. As we entered a deep state of relaxation, I had a vision of a friend's car accident. The imagery was so vivid that it jolted me out of meditation. Concerned, I immediately contacted my friend, urging caution. Later that day, she called to tell me that she narrowly avoided a collision thanks to my warning.

This event solidified my belief in the potential of psychic phenomena. It wasn't about predicting the future but tuning into the subtle energies that connect us all. Over time, I learned to trust my intuition, using it to guide my decisions and help others. My journey has been one of self-discovery and service, revealing that our minds hold incredible potential when we dare to explore beyond the ordinary.

The Power of Collective Consciousness: Uniting Minds for Global Change

By Daniel Kim

As a sociologist, I was fascinated by the concept of collective consciousness the shared beliefs and moral attitudes that operate as a unifying force within society. My academic pursuits, however, were purely theoretical until a personal experience transformed my understanding of human potential.

In 2012, I participated in a global meditation event aimed at fostering peace during a time of international tension. Millions of people from diverse backgrounds synchronized their intentions for one hour. Skeptical but curious, I joined a local group to observe the phenomenon firsthand.

During the meditation, I felt an overwhelming sense of unity and peace. It was as if individual identities dissolved, giving way to a collective heartbeat. The atmosphere was electric yet calming, and I emerged from the experience profoundly moved.

Intrigued, I delved into research on the effects of mass meditation and collective intention. Studies from the Global Consciousness Project indicated that focused collective attention could influence random number generators, suggesting a measurable impact on physical systems. Moreover, periods of synchronized global meditation correlated with temporary reductions in violence and crime rates.

Inspired, I began organizing community events centered around collective intention. One initiative involved gathering volunteers to focus on healing local environmental issues. After several sessions, participants reported increased biodiversity in nearby parks and cleaner waterways anecdotal evidence, but compelling nonetheless.

These experiences shifted my perspective from academic detachment to active participation. I realized that collective consciousness isn't just a sociological concept but a tangible force that can effect real-world change. By uniting minds and hearts, we tap into a wellspring of potential that transcends individual limitations.

Unlocking Superhuman Abilities: The Path of the Yogi

By Ravi Patel

Born into a family with a rich heritage of yoga and meditation, I was exposed to spiritual practices from an early age. However, like many young people, I was more interested in modern pursuits than ancient traditions. It wasn't until a personal crisis in my late twenties that I turned inward, seeking solace and answers.

I embarked on a journey to the Himalayas, studying under a revered yogi who taught me the profound depths of human potential. Through rigorous discipline meditation, breath control (pranayama), and physical postures (asanas) I began to experience changes that defied conventional understanding.

One of the most remarkable abilities I developed was the conscious control of my autonomic bodily functions. I could slow down my heartbeat, regulate my body temperature, and enter deep states of consciousness at will. During one meditation retreat, I remained submerged in icy water for an extended period without any signs of hypothermia a feat that astonished medical professionals who later examined me.

These practices also heightened my senses and cognitive

abilities. My memory improved dramatically, and I could process complex information with ease. But beyond these "superhuman" abilities, the most significant transformation was the profound sense of inner peace and connection to the universe.

Returning to society, I dedicated myself to teaching others how to unlock their potential. I realized that these abilities are not exclusive to mystics or ascetics but are accessible to anyone willing to commit to the path. Through workshops and seminars, I have guided countless individuals in discovering their innate capacities, demonstrating that the boundaries of human potential are far broader than commonly believed.

Transcending Limitations: A Neuroscientist's Exploration of Neuroplasticity

By Dr. Elena Martinez

As a neuroscientist, I was trained to view the brain as a complex but largely fixed organ its capabilities and limitations defined by genetics and early development. However, my research into neuroplasticity challenged these assumptions and opened my eyes to the incredible adaptability of the human mind.

Working with stroke patients, I observed how some individuals recovered functions that were thought to be permanently lost. The brain, it seemed, could rewire itself in response to new challenges and stimuli. Intrigued, I began experimenting with neurofeedback and cognitive training techniques to enhance brain performance in healthy individuals.

One of my most compelling cases involved a middle-aged man who, after practicing specific mental exercises, developed what could be described as photographic memory. He could recall intricate details from conversations, books, and experiences with astonishing accuracy. Functional MRI scans revealed increased connectivity in areas associated with memory and cognition.

These findings led me to explore the potential of unlocking "dormant" areas of the brain. Through a combination of meditation, visualization, and targeted cognitive tasks, participants in my studies demonstrated enhanced creativity, problem-solving skills, and even sensory perception.

My research suggests that the limitations we perceive are often self-imposed or culturally reinforced. By challenging these beliefs and engaging in practices that promote neuroplasticity, we can expand our mental capacities far beyond conventional boundaries. This has profound implications not just for individual development but for society as a whole, as we begin to tap into the vast reservoir of human potential.

PRACTICAL APPLICATIONS AND ACTION STEPS

Activating Your Latent Abilities: A Guide to Unlocking Human Potential

The journey to unlocking human potential is deeply personal yet universally accessible. Whether you're seeking to enhance your intuition, connect with others on a deeper level, or expand your cognitive abilities, there are practical steps you can take to begin this transformative process.

Cultivate Mindfulness and Meditation

- **Daily Practice**: Set aside at least 20 minutes each day for meditation. Focus on your breath, allowing thoughts to pass without judgment. Over time, this practice enhances self-awareness and mental clarity.

- **Mindfulness in Action**: Incorporate mindfulness into everyday activities eating, walking, or even washing dishes. Pay attention to the sensations and experiences in the present moment.

Develop Your Intuition

- **Listen to Your Gut Feelings**: Pay attention to subtle feelings or hunches. Before making decisions, take a moment to tune into your inner guidance.

- **Journaling**: Keep a journal of intuitive impressions and any synchronicities you notice. Reflecting on these entries can help you recognize patterns and strengthen your intuition.

Engage in Energy Work

- **Qi Gong and Tai Chi**: These practices cultivate life-force energy (Qi) through movement and breath control, enhancing vitality and energetic sensitivity.

- **Reiki and Healing Touch**: Explore energy healing modalities that promote balance and healing in yourself and others.

Practice Visualization and Affirmations

- **Creative Visualization**: Imagine desired outcomes vividly, engaging all your senses. This technique can help manifest goals and enhance cognitive abilities.

- **Positive Affirmations**: Use affirmations to reprogram limiting beliefs. Repeat statements like "I am open to my highest potential" to reinforce positive self-perception.

Explore Neuroplasticity Techniques

- **Brain Training Exercises**: Engage in activities that challenge your brain learning a new language, playing musical instruments, or solving puzzles.

- **Mindfulness-Based Stress Reduction (MBSR)**: This program combines mindfulness and yoga to reduce stress and promote neuroplastic changes in the brain.

Foster Emotional Intelligence

- **Empathy Development**: Practice active listening and try to understand others' perspectives without judgment.

- **Emotional Regulation**: Learn techniques to manage emotions effectively, such as deep breathing or cognitive reframing.

Participate in Collective Consciousness Activities

- **Group Meditations**: Join local or online meditation groups to experience the amplified effects of collective intention.

- **Community Service**: Engage in acts of kindness and service, strengthening the sense of interconnectedness.

Enhance Physical Well-being

- **Nutrition**: Fuel your body with nutrient-rich foods that support brain health, such as omega-3 fatty acids, antioxidants, and vitamins.

- **Exercise**: Regular physical activity improves cognitive function and emotional well-being.

Practice Lucid Dreaming and Astral Projection

- **Dream Journaling**: Record your dreams upon waking to enhance dream recall and identify patterns.

- **Lucid Dreaming Techniques**: Use reality checks and intention setting to become conscious within your dreams, exploring the depths of your subconscious mind.

Embrace Continuous Learning and Curiosity

- **Read Widely**: Expand your knowledge across various fields science, philosophy, arts to stimulate creativity and innovation.

- **Attend Workshops and Seminars**: Participate in events that focus on personal development, spirituality, or specialized skills.

Reflection Exercise

Consider the following questions to deepen your understanding of your potential:

- **What innate abilities or interests have you felt drawn to but haven't fully explored?**

- **How might unlocking these abilities enhance your life and contribute to your community?**

- **What steps can you take today to begin nurturing these latent potentials?**

Call to Action

Unlocking human potential is not just a personal endeavor; it's a collective journey that can elevate humanity as a whole. By committing to your growth, you inspire others to do the same, creating a ripple effect of empowerment and transformation.

- **Set Intentions**: Clearly define what abilities or areas you wish to develop.

- **Take Action**: Begin with small, consistent steps. Consistency is key to progress.

- **Connect with Others**: Seek out communities or mentors

who can support and guide you.

- **Share Your Journey**: Your experiences can motivate and guide others on their paths.

Final Thoughts

Human potential is vast and largely untapped. The stories and practices shared in this chapter illustrate that extraordinary abilities are within reach when we open ourselves to possibilities beyond conventional limits.

By embracing practices that enhance mindfulness, intuition, and connection, we not only transform ourselves but also contribute to the evolution of collective consciousness. Each step taken towards unlocking our potential brings us closer to a world where the extraordinary becomes the norm, and the full spectrum of human capabilities is realized.

May your journey be filled with discovery, growth, and the joy of unfolding into the fullness of who you are meant to be.

PART VII: THE PATH AHEAD-EMBRACING THE POWER OF HIDDEN KNOWLEDGE

CHAPTER 14: THE AWAKENING-HOW HIDDEN KNOWLEDGE CAN TRANSFORM OUR FUTURE

"The greatest secret is not what we don't know, but what we fail to see within ourselves. The power to change the world lies in the hands of those who dare to look beyond the veil and embrace the mysteries that connect us all."

Dr. Elias Verne

Prologue

As we stand on the threshold of a new era, the knowledge of the past, once hidden and suppressed, is slowly resurfacing. From the ancient wisdom of lost civilizations to the profound implications of quantum physics, humanity is awakening to the realization that we are more than passive inhabitants of the Earth we are active participants in the cosmos, with the power to shape our own destiny. This chapter explores how embracing the hidden knowledge of humanity can lead to a transformative future, one where technology, spirituality, and human potential are harmoniously integrated. Dr. Elias Verne, a futurist and philosopher, guides us through the possibilities that await, urging us to use the insights of the past to create a future that reflects our highest aspirations.

The Power of Collective Awakening: Humanity at a Crossroads

Humanity is at a critical juncture. The rapid acceleration of technology, environmental challenges, and social upheaval are driving a global awakening. As we reconnect with ancient wisdom and explore the boundaries of science and spirituality, we are presented with a choice: to continue down the path of division and exploitation or to embrace a new paradigm of unity, compassion, and conscious evolution.

The Role of Technology in the New Age

- **Reclaiming Technology for Human Flourishing**
  Technology has the potential to either enslave or liberate humanity, depending on how it is used. The dark side of technological advancement surveillance, disinformation, and environmental degradation reminds us of the importance of ethical stewardship. However, when aligned with conscious intent, technology can be a force for good, enhancing our ability to connect, create, and solve the world's most pressing problems. Innovations like AI, renewable energy, and biotechnology hold the promise of a future where technology works in harmony with nature, supporting human flourishing rather than undermining it.

- **Decentralization and the Rise of Digital Empowerment**
  The emergence of blockchain technology, decentralized networks, and digital currencies represents a shift toward a more democratized and transparent world. These technologies allow individuals to reclaim control over their data, finances, and interactions, bypassing traditional power structures. Decentralization empowers communities to self-govern, collaborate, and build resilient systems that prioritize human values over corporate profits. This movement reflects the broader trend of seeking freedom from centralized control, aligning with the spiritual principle of self-sovereignty.

- **The Fusion of Science and Spirit: Biohacking and Conscious Tech**
  The rise of biohacking using technology to optimize the body and mind blurs the line between biology and technology, opening new frontiers in human potential. From brainwave entrainment devices to wearables that monitor and enhance health, biohacking integrates the physical and the digital, offering tools for self-improvement and self-awareness. As this field evolves, it increasingly incorporates ancient practices such as meditation, breathwork, and energy healing, creating a fusion of science and spirituality that honors both the material and metaphysical aspects of human existence.

The Spiritual Renaissance: Rediscovering Ancient Wisdom

- **The Return to Nature and Sacred Practices**
  A growing movement toward reconnecting with nature and embracing sacred practices is sweeping across the globe. People are rediscovering ancient healing modalities, such as herbal medicine, sound therapy, and shamanic journeying, as complements to modern medical approaches. This return to nature reflects a longing for balance and a recognition that the Earth itself

is a living entity with which we are deeply intertwined. Sacred practices help us reconnect with the rhythms of the natural world, reminding us of the importance of living in harmony with all life.

- ### The Rebirth of Mysticism: Integrating Esoteric Knowledge

Mysticism, once relegated to the fringes of religious traditions, is experiencing a renaissance as people seek direct, personal experiences of the divine. Esoteric knowledge, from Kabbalah to Hermeticism, offers paths to self-realization that transcend dogma and invite seekers to explore the mysteries of existence on their own terms. As more individuals turn inward, guided by ancient teachings and modern insights, a new spiritual paradigm is emerging one that honors the unique journey of each soul while celebrating our collective quest for truth.

- ### Unity Consciousness: The Emergence of a New Spirituality

The concept of unity consciousness the idea that we are all expressions of a single, interconnected source resonates with both spiritual teachings and quantum theories of interconnectedness. This emerging spirituality transcends traditional boundaries, drawing on insights from multiple traditions to create a holistic, inclusive view of the universe. As more people awaken to this perspective, the potential for global healing, cooperation, and collective transformation grows. Unity consciousness invites us to see beyond the illusion of separation and recognize our shared humanity, fostering a sense of kinship that can bridge divides and heal wounds.

Harnessing Collective Intention: The Power to Shape Reality

- ### The Conscious Co-Creation of Society

As we awaken to our roles as co-creators of reality, the potential to consciously shape our societies becomes clear. Movements advocating for regenerative agriculture, sustainable urban design, and community-led governance reflect a desire to build systems that are resilient, just, and aligned with the natural world. Conscious co-creation encourages us to take responsibility for the impact of our actions, choices, and beliefs, understanding that the world we create reflects the collective state of our consciousness.

- **Global Meditation and Collective Healing**
  The power of collective intention has been demonstrated through global meditation events, where millions of people focus their thoughts on peace, healing, or specific global challenges. Studies have shown that these synchronized efforts can have measurable effects on social indicators, such as reduced violence or increased harmony. By harnessing the power of the collective mind, we can create ripples of positive change that extend far beyond individual efforts, illustrating the profound impact of unity in action.

- **Visionary Leadership: Guiding the Way Forward**
  Visionary leaders those who blend wisdom, compassion, and a deep understanding of humanity's interconnectedness are crucial in guiding the transition to a new paradigm. Whether in politics, business, or community organizing, these leaders inspire by example, demonstrating that true power lies not in domination but in service to the greater good. Visionary leadership calls for a redefinition of success, one that prioritizes well-being, sustainability, and the elevation of human potential.

The Path to a New Humanity: Embracing Hidden Knowledge as a Blueprint for the Future

The hidden knowledge explored throughout this book suppressed technologies, ancient wisdom, and untapped human abilities provides a blueprint for the future of humanity. By embracing these insights, we can transcend the limitations of the past and step boldly into a new era of possibility. This path requires courage, curiosity, and a willingness to challenge the status quo, but the rewards are profound: a world where science and spirituality coexist, where human potential is fully realized, and where the mysteries of the universe are not feared but celebrated.

The Integration of Mind, Body, and Spirit

- **Holistic Education: Cultivating the Whole Human**
  The future of education lies in cultivating not just the intellect but the whole human being mind, body, and spirit. Holistic education emphasizes experiential learning, emotional intelligence, and the development of intuition and creativity. By incorporating mindfulness, meditation, and esoteric studies into traditional curricula, we can empower the next generation to navigate the complexities of the modern world with wisdom and grace.

- **The Healing Revolution: Integrative Medicine and Beyond**
  Integrative medicine, which combines conventional treatments with complementary therapies, reflects a growing recognition of the mind-body connection. As research continues to validate the effectiveness of holistic approaches, such as acupuncture, energy healing, and dietary therapies, the medical field is slowly shifting toward a more comprehensive view of health. This healing revolution acknowledges that true well-being encompasses physical, mental, and spiritual dimensions, offering a model of care that is patient-centered and personalized.

- **The Rise of Conscious Communities**
  Around the world, intentional communities are forming that prioritize sustainable living, shared resources, and collective well-being. These conscious communities experiment with new ways of being, from eco-villages focused on permaculture to urban cooperatives that redefine work-life balance. They serve as microcosms of the world we wish to create, providing proof that alternative models of living are not only possible but thriving. By fostering cooperation, inclusivity, and a deep connection to the land, these communities offer hope for a more harmonious future.

Reawakening the Spirit of Innovation

- **Rediscovering Suppressed Technologies for a Sustainable Future**
  Technologies once considered fringe or dangerous, such as free energy devices, water purification systems, and alternative propulsion methods, hold the key to a sustainable future. As barriers to innovation fall, there is an opportunity to revisit these suppressed technologies, refining and integrating them into mainstream use. Rediscovery and reintegration of these innovations could revolutionize how we live, travel, and interact with our environment, creating a world where resource scarcity and environmental degradation are relics of the past.

- **Open Science and Collaborative Research**
  The open science movement, which promotes the sharing of data, methods, and results, represents a shift toward transparency and collaboration in research. By breaking down silos and encouraging interdisciplinary cooperation, open science accelerates discovery and democratizes knowledge. Collaborative research initiatives, often driven by citizen scientists, challenge traditional hierarchies and empower individuals to

contribute to scientific progress, reflecting a collective drive to push the boundaries of human understanding.

- **The Next Frontier: Conscious Technology**

  As our understanding of consciousness deepens, a new wave of technology is emerging that seeks to enhance human potential rather than replace it. Conscious technologies, such as brain-computer interfaces, neural feedback systems, and virtual reality meditation platforms, offer tools for self-exploration and personal growth. These innovations are designed not just to entertain or inform but to elevate the human experience, supporting the development of mindfulness, empathy, and expanded awareness.

Conclusion: Embracing the Unknown, Creating the Future

The hidden secrets of humanity, once the domain of mystics and visionaries, are now coming to light, inviting us to reconsider what is possible. As we embrace these insights, we are reminded that the greatest journey lies not in exploring distant galaxies but in delving into the uncharted territories of our own consciousness. The future is not predetermined; it is a canvas on which we can paint our highest aspirations and deepest truths.

By integrating the wisdom of the past with the discoveries of the present, we can forge a new path one that honors the interconnectedness of all life, celebrates the power of human potential, and reflects the boundless creativity of the cosmos. In this vision of the future, science and spirituality, technology and nature, and individuality and collective consciousness coexist in harmony, guiding us toward a world where the hidden secrets of humanity are not just uncovered but lived.

"The secrets we seek are not beyond our reach; they are within us, waiting to be awakened. The greatest discovery of all is not in what we uncover but in who we become."
Dr. Elias Verne

Reflection Questions:

> **How can the integration of suppressed knowledge, ancient wisdom, and modern innovation shape the future of humanity?**

> **In what ways can individuals contribute to the collective awakening and co-creation of a harmonious, enlightened world?**

> **What steps can you take today to unlock your own potential and embrace the hidden mysteries that connect us all?**

PERSONAL REFLECTIONS AND TESTIMONIES

A Journey of Integration: Bridging Science and Spirituality

By Dr. Emily Harper

As a neuroscientist and lifelong skeptic, I approached the topics of esoteric knowledge and human potential with caution. My world was one of empirical data and measurable outcomes. However, a profound personal experience challenged my perceptions and set me on a transformative journey.

It began during a sabbatical in India, where I sought respite from the pressures of academia. Immersed in a culture rich with spiritual traditions, I found myself attending a lecture on consciousness and its relationship to the brain. The speaker discussed concepts like the interconnectedness of all life and the power of meditation to alter neural pathways ideas that resonated with the fringes of my own research on neuroplasticity.

Intrigued, I decided to participate in a ten-day silent meditation retreat. The experience was both challenging and enlightening. In the silence, I confronted aspects of myself I had long ignored. I became acutely aware of the constant chatter of my mind and the subconscious patterns driving my behavior.

By the end of the retreat, I noticed subtle but significant changes. My stress levels had decreased, my focus improved, and I felt a newfound sense of clarity and purpose. Upon returning to my work, I began integrating mindfulness practices into my research on cognitive function and mental health.

Collaborating with colleagues from diverse disciplines, we explored how ancient meditation techniques could enhance brain health, reduce anxiety, and improve overall well-being. Our studies showed that participants who engaged in regular mindfulness practices exhibited measurable changes in brain structure and function.

This journey taught me that bridging science and spirituality is not only possible but can lead to groundbreaking advancements in understanding the human mind. By embracing hidden knowledge from various cultures and traditions, we can enrich scientific inquiry and unlock new potentials for healing and growth.

Empowering Communities Through Shared Wisdom

By Carlos Mendoza

Growing up in a tight-knit community in Mexico, I was surrounded by stories and traditions passed down through generations. These tales were more than folklore; they were repositories of wisdom that guided our way of life. As I moved to the city for education and career opportunities, I felt disconnected from this heritage.

Years later, working as a social worker in underserved urban areas, I recognized a common thread people felt isolated and disempowered, lacking a sense of identity and belonging. Remembering the strength derived from my own cultural roots, I began to explore how reconnecting with ancestral knowledge could empower individuals and communities.

I organized workshops that combined storytelling, traditional arts, and communal activities. We invited elders to share their experiences and wisdom, fostering intergenerational connections. These gatherings reignited a sense of pride and cohesion within the community.

One remarkable outcome was the revival of traditional agriculture practices. By integrating modern sustainable techniques with ancestral methods, residents transformed vacant lots into thriving community gardens. This not only provided fresh produce but also became a source of communal pride and a catalyst for further positive change.

Witnessing the transformative power of shared wisdom affirmed my belief that embracing our collective heritage can address contemporary challenges. By honoring the knowledge of the past and adapting it to modern contexts, we can build resilient, empowered communities.

Harnessing Technology for Conscious Evolution

By Aisha Thompson

As a software engineer in Silicon Valley, I was at the forefront of technological innovation. Yet, despite the excitement of working on cutting-edge projects, I couldn't shake the feeling that something was missing. Technology was advancing rapidly, but to what end? I began questioning how our creations were impacting humanity on a deeper level.

This introspection led me to explore the concept of conscious technology tools designed not just for efficiency or entertainment but to enhance human potential and well-being. I became involved with a startup focused on developing apps that promote mindfulness, emotional intelligence, and social connection.

One project that stands out was an app that facilitated global meditation events. Users could synchronize their meditation sessions, creating a virtual collective consciousness. The app provided real-time data on participation and allowed users to share experiences, fostering a sense of global community.

Feedback from users was overwhelmingly positive. Many reported feeling more connected, peaceful, and motivated to engage in altruistic activities. This reinforced my belief that technology, when aligned with human values, can be a powerful catalyst for positive change.

I now advocate for ethical tech development, emphasizing the importance of designing with intention and awareness of the broader implications. By aligning technological advancement with the goal of conscious evolution, we can create tools that not only solve problems but also elevate the human experience.

PRACTICAL APPLICATIONS AND ACTION STEPS

Embracing Hidden Knowledge for Personal and Collective Transformation

The journey ahead invites us to integrate the wisdom gleaned from ancient traditions, cutting-edge science, and personal exploration. By embracing hidden knowledge, we can unlock new potentials within ourselves and contribute to a more harmonious and enlightened world. Here are practical steps to guide this transformative process:

Cultivate Lifelong Learning

Diverse Reading: Engage with literature from various disciplines philosophy, science, spirituality, and culture. This broadens perspectives and fosters integrative thinking.

- **Online Courses and Workshops**: Participate in educational programs that explore topics like mindfulness, ethical technology, sustainability, and intercultural studies.

- **Critical Thinking**: Develop the ability to analyze information thoughtfully, recognizing biases and assessing evidence to form balanced views.

Integrate Mindfulness and Self-Reflection

- **Daily Mindfulness Practice**: Incorporate meditation, yoga, or mindful breathing exercises into your routine to enhance self-awareness and emotional regulation.

- **Journaling**: Reflect on personal experiences, insights, and growth. Journaling can help process emotions and track personal development over time.

- **Mindful Technology Use**: Set intentions for how you engage with digital devices, promoting conscious consumption and reducing distractions.

Foster Community and Connection

- **Cultural Exchange**: Participate in community events that celebrate diverse traditions and promote mutual understanding.

- **Volunteerism**: Engage in service projects that address local needs, fostering a sense of purpose and connection to others.

- **Discussion Groups**: Join or form groups focused on exploring philosophical, spiritual, or scientific topics, encouraging open dialogue and shared learning.

Advocate for Ethical Practices

- **Support Ethical Businesses**: Choose to purchase from companies that prioritize sustainability, fair labor practices, and social responsibility.

- **Promote Transparency**: Encourage organizations and institutions to operate openly, fostering trust and accountability.

- **Ethical Technology**: Advocate for the development and use of technology that respects privacy, enhances well-being, and serves the greater good.

Embrace Sustainable Living

- **Environmental Stewardship**: Adopt practices that reduce environmental impact, such as recycling, conserving energy, and supporting renewable resources.

- **Conscious Consumption**: Be mindful of the resources you use and the waste you produce, opting for sustainable and ethical products.

- **Community Gardening**: Participate in or initiate local gardening projects to promote food security and environmental awareness.

Explore Interdisciplinary Approaches

- **Holistic Health**: Combine conventional medicine with complementary practices like acupuncture, nutrition, and stress management for a comprehensive approach to well-being.

- **Collaborative Innovation**: Work across disciplines to solve complex problems, integrating perspectives from science, art, humanities, and technology.

- **Educational Reform**: Advocate for curricula that include emotional intelligence, ethics, and global citizenship alongside traditional academics.

Nurture Creativity and Expression

- **Artistic Pursuits**: Engage in creative activities music, art, writing that allow for self-expression and exploration of inner landscapes.

- **Storytelling**: Share personal narratives and listen to others' stories to build empathy and understanding.

- **Innovation Spaces**: Support or create environments where experimentation and creative thinking are encouraged.

Practice Global Citizenship

- **Stay Informed**: Keep abreast of global issues, understanding how local actions can have worldwide impacts.

- **Cultural Sensitivity**: Approach interactions with people from different backgrounds with respect and openness, valuing diversity.

- **Collective Action**: Participate in movements or initiatives that address global challenges like climate change, poverty, and inequality.

Develop Emotional and Social Intelligence

- **Active Listening**: Practice fully engaging with others when they speak, fostering deeper connections and understanding.

- **Conflict Resolution**: Learn and apply techniques to navigate disagreements constructively, promoting harmony in relationships.

- **Empathy Exercises**: Regularly put yourself in others' shoes to appreciate different perspectives and experiences.

10. Embody Purpose and Vision

- **Set Intentional Goals**: Define what you wish to achieve personally and how it aligns with contributing to the greater good.

- **Align Actions with Values**: Ensure that daily choices reflect your core beliefs and the impact you wish to have on the world.

- **Mentorship and Leadership**: Guide and inspire others through your actions, sharing knowledge and supporting their journeys.

Reflection Exercise

Consider how embracing hidden knowledge can transform your life and community:

- **What areas of hidden knowledge resonate most with you, and why?**

- **How can you integrate this knowledge into your personal or professional life to create positive change?**

- **What steps can you take to share these insights with others, fostering collective growth?**

Call to Action

The path ahead beckons us to move beyond passive acceptance of the status quo and actively engage in shaping a better future. By embracing the power of hidden knowledge, we tap into a wellspring of wisdom that can guide us toward more fulfilling lives and a more harmonious world.

- **Begin Today**: Choose one action from the list above to implement in your life this week.

- **Connect with Others**: Reach out to friends, family, or colleagues to share your journey and invite collaboration.

- **Stay Committed**: Recognize that transformation is an ongoing process requiring patience, dedication, and resilience.

CONCLUSION: A NEW ERA OF CONSCIOUS EVOLUTION

As we stand at the threshold of a new era, the convergence of ancient wisdom and modern innovation offers unprecedented opportunities for growth. The hidden knowledge that once seemed distant or inaccessible is now within our grasp, inviting us to explore, integrate, and apply it in transformative ways.

By embracing this knowledge, we not only unlock our individual potentials but also contribute to the collective evolution of humanity. Each step we take towards understanding and embodying these truths ripples outward, influencing our communities and the world at large.

Let us move forward with curiosity, compassion, and courage, knowing that the journey ahead is as much about the discoveries we make as it is about the people we become along the way. Together, we can forge a path that honors the richness of our shared heritage and paves the way for a future filled with possibility and promise.

"The real voyage of discovery consists not in seeking new landscapes, but in having new eyes."
Marcel Proust

PART VIII:
THE COSMIC
CONNECTION
HUMANITY'S ROLE
IN THE GREATER
UNIVERSE

CHAPTER 15:
THE COSMIC CONNECTION UNDERSTANDING HUMANITY'S PLACE IN THE VASTNESS OF THE UNIVERSE

"The universe is not a cold, indifferent expanse; it is a living, conscious entity, and we are an intrinsic part of its grand design. To understand our role in the cosmos is to awaken to the profound truth that we are the universe experiencing itself."

Dr. Lydia Cole

Prologue

From the earliest stargazers to the most advanced astrophysicists, humanity has always looked to the heavens with a mixture of awe, curiosity, and a deep, unspoken sense of connection. For millennia, we have wondered about our place in the vast expanse of the cosmos, seeking answers in myths, mathematics, and metaphysics. But what if the universe is not just an empty stage upon which life randomly appears? What if it is a conscious, interconnected system in which humanity plays a vital role? Dr. Lydia Cole, an expert in cosmic consciousness, takes us on an extraordinary journey into the heart of the universe, exploring how our existence is intertwined with the stars, the galaxies, and the very fabric of space and time. This chapter reveals that understanding our cosmic connection is not just an intellectual endeavor it is a transformative realization that can reshape how we view ourselves and our place in the grand scheme of existence.

The Living Universe: A Conscious, Interconnected Cosmos

Recent advancements in science, coupled with ancient spiritual insights, are converging to suggest that the universe is far more than a mechanical system governed by impersonal laws. Instead, it appears to be a living, conscious entity, with every particle, planet, and person playing a crucial part in the cosmic symphony.

The Anthropic Principle: The Universe Fine-Tuned for Life

- **Fine-Tuning and the Multiverse Theory**
  The Anthropic Principle posits that the universe's fundamental constants such as the strength of gravity, the charge of the electron, and the cosmological constant are precisely calibrated to allow the existence of life. Even the slightest deviation in these values would render the universe inhospitable, suggesting that the conditions necessary for life are not mere accidents. Some physicists propose the multiverse theory, where countless universes exist, each with different physical laws, and we happen to inhabit the one that supports life. However, this theory

also hints at a deeper, almost intentional design behind existence, one that resonates with ancient beliefs about a purposeful cosmos.

- **The Goldilocks Zone and the Search for Exoplanets**
  Our solar system's location in the Milky Way, Earth's precise distance from the sun, and the protective presence of gas giants like Jupiter all contribute to the conditions that make life possible here. Known as the "Goldilocks Zone," this delicate balance is mirrored in the discovery of thousands of exoplanets in habitable zones around other stars. These findings suggest that life-supporting planets may be common, reinforcing the idea that the universe is inherently life-friendly, almost as if it is designed to nurture consciousness.

- **The Role of Dark Matter and Dark Energy**
  Despite making up over 95% of the universe, dark matter and dark energy remain some of the greatest mysteries in modern physics. These unseen forces not only influence the structure of the cosmos but may also play a role in the emergence and evolution of life. Some speculative theories propose that dark matter could interact with consciousness in ways we do not yet understand, hinting at a cosmic web that connects all matter, energy, and awareness.

The Gaia Hypothesis: Earth as a Living Being

- **The Planetary Consciousness of Gaia**
  Proposed by scientist James Lovelock, the Gaia Hypothesis views Earth as a self-regulating, living system where the biosphere, atmosphere, oceans, and land interact to maintain conditions favorable for life. This theory suggests that life is not a passive occupant of Earth but an active participant in shaping its environment. Gaia is

not just a poetic metaphor but a scientific model that sees our planet as a complex, conscious entity, responding dynamically to changes and threats.

- **Sacred Ecology: Ancient Wisdom Meets Modern Science**
Many Indigenous cultures have long regarded Earth as a sentient being, known by names like Pachamama, Mother Earth, or the Great Spirit. These traditions emphasize a relationship of respect, reciprocity, and reverence with the natural world, echoing the principles of the Gaia Hypothesis. Modern ecological science is beginning to validate these ancient perspectives, recognizing that ecosystems function as interconnected webs of life, where every species, including humans, plays a vital role in maintaining balance.

- **Earth's Energy Grids and Ley Lines**
The concept of Earth's energy grids and ley lines paths of concentrated energy that crisscross the planet further supports the idea of a living Earth. These grids are believed to connect sacred sites, such as Stonehenge, the Pyramids of Giza, and Machu Picchu, forming a planetary network of spiritual and energetic significance. Some researchers suggest that ancient civilizations were aware of these grids and built their monuments accordingly, aligning them with the natural energy flow of the Earth. This alignment reflects a profound understanding of the planet's living essence and our place within it.

The Conscious Cosmos: New Theories of a Living Universe

- **Biocentrism: Consciousness Creates the Cosmos**
Biocentrism, a theory proposed by scientist Robert Lanza, posits that life and consciousness are not mere byproducts of the universe but are fundamental to its existence. According to this view, the universe arises from consciousness rather than the other way around. Time, space, and even the physical laws are seen as constructs

shaped by the observer. This theory aligns with spiritual teachings that view the cosmos as a manifestation of a universal mind or divine consciousness, suggesting that life is not an accident but an essential aspect of reality.

- **The Holographic Universe: The Cosmos as a Projection of Mind**
  The holographic principle suggests that the entire universe can be understood as a vast, multidimensional projection, where every part contains information about the whole. This model not only challenges conventional notions of space and time but also supports the idea of a conscious universe where everything is interconnected. If the universe functions as a hologram, then every thought, action, and intention has a ripple effect, influencing the entire system in ways that we are only beginning to comprehend.

- **Quantum Consciousness and the Cosmic Web**
  Quantum physics reveals that the universe operates on principles of interconnectedness, non-locality, and uncertainty, blurring the lines between observer and observed. The concept of quantum consciousness suggests that the entire cosmos is imbued with a form of awareness, and that what we perceive as reality is a co-creation between the universe and our consciousness. This theory implies that the cosmos is not a detached observer but a participatory force, constantly interacting with and responding to conscious beings.

The Extraterrestrial Connection: Humanity and the Greater Galactic Family

As we explore the possibility of life beyond Earth, the question arises: Are we alone in the universe, or are we part of a vast community of conscious beings spread across the stars? The search for extraterrestrial life, once confined to science fiction, is now a legitimate scientific pursuit, with profound implications for our understanding of ourselves and our place in the cosmos.

The Search for Extraterrestrial Intelligence (SETI)

• **Listening to the Stars: The SETI Project**
For decades, the Search for Extraterrestrial Intelligence (SETI) has been scanning the skies for radio signals or other forms of communication from intelligent civilizations. Although definitive contact has yet to be made, the discovery of potentially habitable exoplanets and unusual cosmic phenomena continues to fuel speculation about the existence of advanced extraterrestrial life. SETI represents humanity's ongoing quest to connect with other conscious beings, reflecting a deep-seated desire to understand our place in the larger galactic community.

• **The Fermi Paradox: Where Is Everybody?**
The Fermi Paradox highlights the contradiction between the high probability of extraterrestrial civilizations and the lack of evidence for their existence. Various theories attempt to explain this paradox, ranging from the idea that advanced civilizations are avoiding us, to the possibility that they exist on a plane of existence we cannot yet perceive. Some suggest that humanity itself is part of a cosmic experiment or quarantine, watched over by more advanced beings who are waiting for us to reach a certain level of consciousness before making contact.

• **The WOW! Signal and Other Anomalies**
In 1977, a strong, unexplained signal dubbed the WOW! Signal was detected by a SETI radio telescope, sparking intense speculation about its origin. While the signal was never repeated, it remains one of the most compelling pieces of evidence suggesting the possibility of extraterrestrial communication. Other anomalies,

such as unexplained radio bursts and unusual cosmic structures, continue to intrigue scientists and hint at the existence of other intelligent life forms, beckoning us to keep searching.

Ancient Alien Theories: Evidence of Past Visitations

- **Ancient Astronauts and Mythological Accounts**
  The theory of ancient astronauts suggests that extraterrestrial beings visited Earth in the distant past, influencing the development of human civilization. Proponents point to mythological accounts, religious texts, and ancient artwork depicting gods descending from the skies, flying machines, and advanced technologies. The legends of the Anunnaki in Sumerian mythology, the Vimanas of ancient India, and the mysterious Dogon tribe's knowledge of the Sirius star system all suggest that early humans may have had contact with beings from beyond our world.

- **Megalithic Mysteries and Advanced Engineering**
  The construction of ancient megalithic sites, such as the Pyramids of Giza, Stonehenge, and Puma Punku, continues to baffle modern engineers. These structures often exhibit precision, scale, and alignment with celestial bodies that seem beyond the capabilities of the civilizations that built them. Some theorists argue that these feats of engineering were accomplished with the assistance of advanced beings who imparted their knowledge of mathematics, astronomy, and technology. Whether these beings were extraterrestrial or from a lost advanced civilization on Earth remains a topic of heated debate.

- **The Nazca Lines and Geoglyphs**
  The Nazca Lines in Peru vast geoglyphs etched into the desert floor depict animals, geometric shapes, and humanoid figures visible only from the sky. The purpose

and method of their creation remain unclear, leading to speculation that they were made as signals or markers for ancient visitors from above. Similar geoglyphs found in other parts of the world suggest a global phenomenon, hinting at a shared knowledge or influence that transcends geographic boundaries.

The Implications of Contact: Preparing for a New Reality

- **Disclosure and the Role of Government Secrecy**
  Governments around the world have long maintained secrecy regarding UFO sightings, alleged alien encounters, and classified research into extraterrestrial phenomena. Recent declassifications of military footage showing unidentified aerial phenomena (UAPs) have reignited public interest and speculation about the reality of extraterrestrial contact. The implications of disclosure are vast, potentially challenging religious beliefs, social structures, and scientific paradigms. As the conversation around extraterrestrial life becomes more mainstream, society must grapple with what it means to share the universe with other intelligent beings.

- **Cosmic Citizenship: Embracing Our Galactic Identity**
  The prospect of contact with extraterrestrial civilizations forces humanity to reconsider its identity on a cosmic scale. No longer confined to national, cultural, or even planetary identities, we are invited to see ourselves as part of a broader galactic family. This shift in perspective calls for a reevaluation of how we treat each other, our planet, and the cosmos. Cosmic citizenship demands responsibility, humility, and a commitment to peace, recognizing that we are not isolated but deeply interconnected with a universe teeming with life.

- **Spiritual and Psychological Preparedness for Contact**
  Contact with extraterrestrial beings, whether in the future or acknowledged as having occurred in the

past, would have profound psychological and spiritual impacts. How would humanity reconcile its place in the universe with the existence of other conscious beings? Preparing for such a revelation involves not just scientific readiness but also spiritual and emotional resilience. It calls for open-mindedness, a willingness to let go of outdated paradigms, and the courage to embrace a new understanding of the cosmos and our role within it.

Conclusion: Humanity's Cosmic Awakening

The exploration of our cosmic connection reveals that humanity is not adrift in an indifferent universe; we are integral to a vast, conscious, and interconnected whole. Whether through the fine-tuned conditions that allow life, the possibility of extraterrestrial contact, or the emerging understanding of a conscious cosmos, we are beginning to see ourselves as part of something far greater than we ever imagined.

This awakening to our cosmic identity invites us to rethink our relationship with the universe, to honor the mysteries that surround us, and to embrace our role as stewards of both Earth and the stars. By recognizing our place in the grand design, we can align our actions, intentions, and innovations with the greater good, creating a future that reflects the highest potentials of a conscious and interconnected humanity.

"We are stardust, born from the same cosmic fire that lights the stars. To understand the universe is to understand ourselves, for we are its eyes, its mind, and its heart."
Dr. Lydia Cole

Reflection Questions:

> **How does the idea of a conscious, interconnected universe change your perception of your role in the cosmos?**

> **What are the implications of potential extraterrestrial contact for humanity, and how can we prepare for this possibility both scientifically and spiritually?**

> **How can embracing our cosmic connection inspire us to live more consciously, sustainably, and compassionately?**

PERSONAL REFLECTIONS AND TESTIMONIES

A Glimpse of Infinity: An Astronaut's Journey Beyond Earth

By Commander Sarah Thompson

As a child gazing up at the night sky from my backyard, I was captivated by the twinkling stars scattered across the velvet darkness. Little did I know that one day I would have the privilege of venturing beyond our planet's atmosphere to witness the cosmos firsthand.

Training as an astronaut was a rigorous journey, but nothing could have prepared me for the profound experience of seeing Earth from space. On my first mission aboard the International Space Station, as we orbited the Earth every 90 minutes, I watched countless sunrises and sunsets paint the horizon with hues beyond imagination.

One evening, floating in the cupola with its panoramic windows, I was struck by a profound realization. The borders that divide nations vanished beneath me, replaced by the seamless curve of our shared home. The interconnectedness of all life became palpable. I felt an overwhelming sense of unity not just with humanity, but with the entire cosmos.

During a spacewalk to repair a module, I paused to look into the depths of space. The silence was absolute, and the stars shone with a brilliance unfiltered by Earth's atmosphere. In that moment, I felt both infinitesimal and integral to the vast tapestry of the universe. It was as if the cosmos was a living entity, and I was a conscious thread woven into its fabric.

Upon returning to Earth, this experience transformed my perspective. I became an advocate for planetary stewardship and the exploration of space not just for scientific advancement, but as a means to foster a deeper connection between humanity and the universe. I believe that by understanding our place in the cosmos, we can transcend the divisions that separate us and work together for the greater good.

Whispers from the Cosmos: An Astrophysicist's Encounter with the Unknown

By Dr. Elena Rodriguez

My fascination with the stars began when I received my first telescope at the age of ten. The mysteries of the universe beckoned, and I dedicated my life to unraveling them. As an astrophysicist, I spent countless nights at observatories, peering deep into space in search of answers.

During a research project aimed at detecting exoplanets, my team observed an unusual signal emanating from a distant star system. The patterns were unlike anything we'd seen before complex, repeating sequences that defied natural explanations. Intrigued, we delved deeper, analyzing the data with every tool at our disposal.

As we decrypted the signal, it became evident that it was not random. The mathematical structures mirrored those found in nature's most intricate designs the Fibonacci sequence, fractals, and golden ratios. It was as if the universe itself was communicating through a cosmic language of mathematics.

This discovery led me to contemplate the possibility of an underlying intelligence woven into the fabric of the cosmos. Could consciousness be a fundamental aspect of the universe, permeating every particle and wave? The idea challenged my scientific beliefs, pushing me beyond the boundaries of conventional thought.

I began exploring the intersection of science and spirituality, studying ancient philosophies that spoke of the universe as a living, conscious entity. My journey led me to understand that science and spirituality are not mutually exclusive but complementary paths to understanding the same ultimate reality.

This paradigm shift transformed my work. I now approach my research with a sense of reverence and wonder, recognizing that in studying the cosmos, we are also exploring the depths of our own consciousness. The stars are no longer distant objects but mirrors reflecting the infinite potential within each of us.

Embracing the Cosmic Symphony: A Mystic's Experience of Universal Unity

By Aiden Walker

My path as a mystic began after a profound spiritual awakening during a meditation retreat in the mountains. Immersed in silence and solitude, I sought to understand the nature of existence and my place within it.

One night, as I meditated under a canopy of stars, I felt a surge of energy coursing through me. It was as if the boundaries of my physical body dissolved, and I became one with the universe. I could sense the pulsating rhythms of celestial bodies, the harmony of galaxies spiraling through space, and the subtle vibrations connecting all forms of life.

This experience was beyond words a direct knowing that everything is interconnected in a cosmic web of consciousness. I realized that separation is an illusion; we are all expressions of the same universal essence manifesting in myriad forms.

Driven to integrate this wisdom into daily life, I traveled the world studying with spiritual teachers and indigenous elders. From the shamans of the Amazon to the sages of the Himalayas, I learned that many cultures hold knowledge of our intrinsic connection to the cosmos.

In my practice, I guide others to experience this unity through meditation, sound healing, and sacred rituals. Witnessing individuals awaken to their cosmic nature is a profound honor. As more people embrace this awareness, we move closer to a collective shift in consciousness a renaissance of the human spirit aligned with the greater universe.

PRACTICAL APPLICATIONS AND ACTION STEPS

Embracing the Cosmic Connection: Steps to Align with the Universe

The understanding that we are an integral part of the cosmos opens doors to profound transformation. By embracing our cosmic connection, we can cultivate a deeper sense of purpose, harmony, and unity. Here are practical steps to integrate this awareness into your life:

Expand Your Perspective

- **Stargazing and Astronomy**: Spend time observing the night sky. Use a telescope or binoculars to explore celestial bodies. Learning about the universe fosters a sense of wonder and places daily concerns into a broader context.

- **Educational Resources**: Engage with documentaries, books, and courses on cosmology, astrophysics, and space exploration. Knowledge deepens appreciation and connection.

Practice Cosmic Mindfulness

- **Meditation**: Incorporate meditations that focus on

cosmic themes. Visualize yourself as part of the universe, connected to all that exists.

- **Breathwork**: Practice breathing techniques that align with natural rhythms, such as the lunar cycle or circadian rhythms, to attune your body to cosmic patterns.

Cultivate Environmental Stewardship

- **Sustainable Living**: Recognize Earth as a precious part of the cosmos. Adopt eco-friendly practices reduce waste, conserve energy, and support sustainable initiatives.

- **Nature Connection**: Spend time in natural settings. Observing the intricacies of ecosystems reinforces the interconnectedness of all life.

Engage in Collective Initiatives

- **Global Meditation Events**: Participate in synchronized meditations or consciousness-raising activities aimed at fostering planetary unity and peace.

- **Support Space Exploration**: Advocate for and support organizations dedicated to space research and exploration, recognizing their role in expanding human understanding.

Integrate Cosmic Wisdom into Daily Life

- **Mindful Technology Use**: Balance technological engagement with mindful practices. Use technology to connect, learn, and share rather than as a distraction.

- **Creative Expression**: Channel cosmic themes into art, music, writing, or other creative outlets. Expressing these ideas can inspire others and deepen your own connection.

Foster Global Community

- **Cultural Exchange**: Engage with people from different backgrounds. Understanding diverse perspectives enriches our collective human experience.

- **Altruism and Compassion**: Practice kindness and empathy. Recognize that every act impacts the whole, contributing to the collective well-being.

Reflect on Personal Purpose

- **Life Purpose Exploration**: Contemplate how your unique talents and passions align with a greater cosmic purpose. Seek ways to contribute positively to the world.

- **Set Intentions**: Align your goals with universal principles such as love, harmony, and unity. Let these guide your decisions and actions.

Reflection Exercise

Take time to contemplate the following questions:

- **How do you perceive your relationship with the universe?**

- **In what ways can recognizing your cosmic connection enhance your life and the lives of others?**

- **What steps can you take to deepen your understanding and experience of this connection?**

Call to Action

Embracing our role in the greater universe is both a personal and collective journey. As you deepen your connection with the cosmos, consider how you can inspire others to do the same.

- **Share Your Experiences**: Discuss your insights and discoveries with friends, family, or through creative outlets.

- **Collaborate on Cosmic Projects**: Join or initiate community projects that promote cosmic awareness, such as astronomy clubs, environmental initiatives, or consciousness-raising events.

- **Live with Cosmic Consciousness**: Let the awareness of your place in the universe inform your daily choices, fostering a life of purpose, harmony, and fulfillment.

FINAL THOUGHTS

The cosmos is not a distant, unattainable expanse but a vibrant tapestry in which we are intimately woven. By acknowledging and embracing our cosmic connection, we unlock the potential for profound personal growth and contribute to the evolution of humanity as a whole.

As we reach for the stars, both literally and metaphorically, we are reminded of our shared origins and destiny. The atoms that compose our bodies were forged in the hearts of ancient stars. In understanding this, we realize that we are not merely inhabitants of the universe we are the universe expressing itself as human beings.

May this awareness inspire you to live with wonder, compassion, and a deep sense of unity with all that exists.

THE PATH FORWARD REFLECTIONS ON THE HIDDEN SECRETS OF HUMANITY AND OUR COLLECTIVE FUTURE

"In seeking the hidden truths of the universe, we are not just uncovering ancient secrets we are rediscovering ourselves. The knowledge we reclaim has the power to change the course of our destiny."

Dr. Armand Valois

Reflections on the Journey Through Hidden Knowledge

The journey through the hidden secrets of humanity has taken us across lost civilizations, suppressed technologies, secret societies, and esoteric symbols each a piece of a grand puzzle that connects us to our past, shapes our present, and influences our future. These secrets, often shrouded in mystery, censorship, or denial, hold the potential to transform our understanding of who we are and what we are capable of achieving.

As we have explored, the hidden powers that shape our world from ancient secret societies to modern technological manipulators are not merely relics of the past but ongoing forces that continue to influence global events. Whether through covert operations, scientific suppression, or the manipulation of knowledge, these forces have sought to control the flow of information, the direction of innovation, and the very fabric of society.

Yet, the hidden knowledge of humanity is not lost; it is simply waiting to be rediscovered. The suppressed technologies, lost wisdom, and esoteric teachings that have been buried throughout history can inspire us to rethink our place in the world, challenge the established order, and forge new paths toward a more enlightened and interconnected future.

The Power of Rediscovery: Knowledge as a Catalyst for Change

Knowledge is power, and hidden knowledge possesses a unique power to disrupt, inspire, and awaken. Throughout history, those who have dared to seek forbidden truths have often been met with resistance, but they have also been the catalysts for profound change. The rediscovery of lost technologies, the revival of ancient wisdom, and the decoding of esoteric symbols can serve as keys to unlocking human potential and addressing the challenges of our time.

Reclaiming Suppressed Technologies and Innovations

- **Innovation Beyond Boundaries**: Suppressed technologies, such as free energy devices, alternative healing methods, and advanced transportation systems, offer pathways to a future that is more sustainable, equitable, and free from the constraints of current power structures. By embracing these innovations, we can challenge the status quo and build systems that prioritize the well-being of people and the planet.

- **The Role of Independent Researchers and Citizen Scientists**: The democratization of knowledge through the internet and open-source platforms allows independent researchers and citizen scientists to explore and develop technologies that were once the domain of well-funded institutions. This grassroots approach to innovation empowers individuals to take control of their own discoveries, bypassing traditional gatekeepers and challenging the monopolies that have historically suppressed breakthrough ideas.

- **A New Paradigm of Collaboration and Transparency**: Moving beyond the competitive, secretive models of the past, the future of innovation lies in collaboration, transparency, and shared knowledge. Open science initiatives, public data repositories, and international cooperation can create an environment where discoveries are shared for the common good rather than hoarded for profit or control. This shift toward openness can accelerate technological advancements and address global challenges more effectively.

Embracing Esoteric Wisdom and Sacred Knowledge

- **The Relevance of Ancient Teachings in Modern Times**: The esoteric knowledge of our ancestors embodied in symbols, sacred geometry, and spiritual teachings offers profound insights into the nature of reality, consciousness, and our connection to the cosmos. By integrating this ancient wisdom into modern life, we can foster a deeper sense of purpose, harmony, and interconnectedness that transcends the materialism and fragmentation of contemporary society.

- **Spiritual Awakening and the Evolution of Consciousness**: The resurgence of interest in sacred geometry, meditation, and holistic healing reflects a growing desire for spiritual awakening and personal transformation. As individuals seek to align with the natural rhythms of the universe, there is a collective shift toward higher consciousness, one that values inner wisdom, environmental stewardship, and the recognition of our shared humanity.

- **Creating Sacred Spaces and Intentional Communities**: Inspired by the principles of sacred geometry and esoteric traditions, many people are creating intentional communities, eco-villages, and spiritual retreats that embody the values of harmony, balance, and sustainability. These spaces serve as living laboratories for new ways of being, where ancient knowledge and modern innovation coexist, offering models for a more compassionate and connected world.

The Challenge of Hidden Power: Confronting the Forces That Shape Our World

While the potential of rediscovered knowledge is immense, the challenge of confronting the hidden powers that shape our world remains daunting. From shadow governments to corporate monopolies, the forces that seek to control information, suppress technologies, and manipulate narratives do so to maintain their dominance. Understanding these forces and their methods is the first step in dismantling their influence and reclaiming our collective future.

The Fight for Transparency and Accountability

- **Exposing Hidden Agendas**: Whistleblowers, investigative journalists, and activists play a crucial role in exposing the hidden agendas of powerful entities. By shining a light on covert operations, scientific suppression, and corporate malfeasance, they hold those in power accountable and inform the public of the true nature of the systems that govern their lives.

- **The Role of Digital Technology in Empowerment and Surveillance**: While digital technology can be a tool for empowerment, it also poses significant risks of surveillance and control. Balancing the benefits of connectivity with the need for privacy, security, and digital rights is essential to preventing the misuse of technology by hidden powers. Advocacy for robust data protection laws, ethical AI development, and transparent algorithms can help safeguard individual freedoms in the digital age.

- **Building Resilient Communities**: The creation of resilient communities whether through local governance, alternative economies, or decentralized technologies can reduce dependence on centralized power structures. By fostering self-sufficiency, mutual aid, and local decision-making, communities can resist the influence of hidden powers and reclaim control over their own destinies.

Reclaiming the Narrative: Education and Public Engagement

- **Educating the Next Generation**: Education is a powerful tool for challenging established narratives and inspiring critical thinking. By teaching young people to question, explore, and seek truth beyond the surface, we empower them to become the changemakers of tomorrow.

Integrating alternative histories, suppressed knowledge, and esoteric teachings into educational curricula can broaden perspectives and ignite a passion for discovery.

- **The Power of Storytelling and Art**: Storytelling, art, and media have the power to shape public perception and spark social change. By reclaiming the narrative from those who manipulate it for control, artists, writers, and filmmakers can inspire new ways of thinking and bring hidden truths to light. Creative expressions that explore the mysteries of existence, challenge dogmas, and celebrate the interconnectedness of life can serve as catalysts for a cultural awakening.

- **Fostering Open Dialogue and Collective Inquiry**: Open dialogue, public forums, and citizen-led initiatives create spaces where people can come together to discuss, debate, and explore complex issues. Encouraging collective inquiry into the mysteries of the universe, the hidden forces that shape our world, and the possibilities of a better future can strengthen the bonds of community and foster a shared sense of purpose.

The Vision of a Transformed World: From Hidden Secrets to Open Truths

As we move forward, the vision of a transformed world a world where knowledge is free, technology serves humanity, and spiritual wisdom guides our actions offers hope for a brighter future. This transformation begins with each of us: in our willingness to seek truth, challenge the status quo, and embrace the mysteries that connect us to the cosmos.

A World Where Knowledge Is Free and Accessible

- **The Open Knowledge Movement**: The rise of open access, open-source technology, and shared research initiatives is a testament to the growing demand for knowledge that is accessible to all. By breaking down barriers to information, we can create a more informed, empowered, and innovative society. The dream of free knowledge is not just a utopian ideal but a practical pathway to solving the world's most pressing problems.

- **Rediscovering Lost Technologies for a Sustainable Future**: Imagine a world powered by clean, limitless energy, where advanced healing technologies are available to all, and sustainable practices guide every aspect of life. Rediscovering and developing suppressed technologies could revolutionize how we live, work, and interact with our environment, paving the way for a more harmonious coexistence with the planet.

- **The Role of Global Collaboration**: Solving global challenges requires global cooperation. By transcending national, ideological, and corporate boundaries, humanity can pool its knowledge and resources to address issues like climate change, poverty, and disease. A future of open collaboration, where discoveries are shared freely and solutions are co-created, is within our reach if we choose to embrace it.

A New Renaissance of Spiritual and Scientific Integration

- **The Convergence of Science and Spirituality**: The divide between science and spirituality is narrowing as new discoveries in quantum physics, neuroscience, and cosmology echo ancient esoteric teachings. Concepts such as the interconnectedness of all things, the power of consciousness, and the nature of reality are being explored through both scientific inquiry and spiritual practice. This convergence offers a holistic view of existence, one that honors both the material and the metaphysical.

- **Creating Sacred Spaces in Modern Life**: The principles

of sacred geometry, harmony, and intentional design can be applied to modern life, creating environments that nurture the soul and reflect the natural rhythms of the universe. From urban planning that prioritizes green spaces and community connections to architecture that incorporates sacred proportions, the integration of esoteric wisdom into everyday life can foster a sense of peace, purpose, and belonging.

- **The Awakening of Global Consciousness**: As humanity faces unprecedented challenges, there is also a growing sense of spiritual awakening. People around the world are seeking deeper meaning, reconnecting with ancient wisdom, and embracing practices that promote inner transformation. This awakening represents a collective shift toward higher consciousness, one that values compassion, empathy, and the recognition of our shared humanity.

Final Thoughts: Embracing the Journey of Discovery

The journey through the hidden secrets of humanity is an invitation to explore, question, and seek beyond the surface. It challenges us to confront the forces that shape our world, reclaim the knowledge that has been suppressed, and embrace the mysteries that connect us to the cosmos. As we continue on this path, we are reminded that the quest for truth is not just an intellectual pursuit but a deeply personal and transformative journey.

The hidden knowledge of humanity is not a relic of the past it is a living legacy that calls us to awaken, evolve, and co-create a future that honors the best of who we are. By embracing this legacy, we can unlock the full potential of our species, heal the divisions that separate us, and step into a new era of collective enlightenment.

"The secrets of humanity are not hidden from us; they are hidden within us. To discover them is to rediscover ourselves."

Dr. Helena Armitage

Reflection Questions:

How can we, as individuals and as a society, work to uncover and share the hidden knowledge that has been suppressed throughout history?

In what ways can the integration of ancient wisdom, suppressed technologies, and modern innovation create a more harmonious and enlightened future?

What role will each of us play in the ongoing journey of discovery, and how can we contribute to a world where knowledge, truth, and the pursuit of understanding are valued above all else?

CONCLUSION: THE DAWN OF A NEW ERA EMBRACING THE HIDDEN SECRETS AND RECLAIMING OUR FUTURE

"The secrets of humanity are not buried in distant lands or locked away in hidden vaults; they are woven into the fabric of our very being, waiting to be rediscovered. The path forward lies in our willingness to explore the unknown, challenge the limits of what we believe is possible, and awaken to the boundless potential within ourselves."

Dr. Helena Armitage

A Journey Through the Hidden Secrets

As we reach the end of our journey through the forbidden

secrets of humanity, we find ourselves standing at a pivotal moment in history. The knowledge we have explored from lost civilizations and suppressed technologies to the mysteries of consciousness and the vastness of the cosmos paints a picture of a world far richer, more complex, and more interconnected than we have been led to believe. These secrets, long hidden and often dismissed, are not merely relics of the past or fringe theories of the present. They are powerful keys that can unlock a future filled with potential, transformation, and enlightenment.

Our exploration has shown that the narrative of human history is far from complete. It is a tapestry woven with threads of ancient wisdom, scientific discovery, and spiritual insight that together reveal a deeper understanding of who we are, where we come from, and where we might be headed. The suppressed technologies that could have reshaped our world, the esoteric knowledge that connects us to the cosmos, and the latent abilities that lie dormant within each of us are all part of a grander design a design that calls us to awaken, evolve, and embrace the extraordinary.

The Power of Rediscovery: Reclaiming Our Lost Heritage

Throughout history, those in power have often sought to control knowledge, suppress innovation, and rewrite the story of humanity in ways that serve their interests. Ancient texts have been hidden, scientific discoveries have been silenced, and spiritual teachings have been distorted. Yet, despite these efforts, the truth has a way of resurfacing. Today, we are witnessing a global awakening a movement to reclaim the knowledge that has been lost, to honor the wisdom of our ancestors, and to integrate these insights into a new vision for the future.

Reviving Ancient Wisdom and Reconnecting with Our Roots

The resurgence of interest in ancient civilizations, sacred sites, and spiritual traditions reflects a deep yearning to reconnect with the wisdom of the past. As we unearth the mysteries of places like Göbekli Tepe, the Pyramids of Giza, and the ancient cities of Lemuria and Atlantis, we are not just discovering stones and artifacts; we are uncovering a forgotten heritage that challenges our understanding of human potential and the nature of reality. These ancient cultures, often dismissed as primitive or mythical, were repositories of advanced knowledge in astronomy, mathematics, medicine, and spirituality. They understood the interconnectedness of all life, the importance of harmony with nature, and the power of the human spirit.

By embracing this heritage, we can learn from the successes and failures of our ancestors, rediscover the technologies and healing practices that have been suppressed, and apply this knowledge to the challenges of our time. The ancient world was not merely a precursor to modern civilization it was a guide, offering us blueprints for living in balance with ourselves, each other, and the planet.

Suppressed Technologies: Reimagining the Possible

One of the most compelling revelations of our journey is the existence of technologies that have been hidden, suppressed, or dismissed as impossible. From Tesla's free energy devices and cold fusion experiments to ancient engineering feats that defy explanation, these technologies challenge the limits of what we believe is achievable. They suggest that humanity has long possessed the tools to create a world of abundance, sustainability, and freedom, but that these tools have been kept from us by those who profit from the status quo.

The rediscovery and development of these technologies could revolutionize every aspect of human life. Imagine a world where energy is free and limitless, where advanced healing methods eradicate disease, and where transportation is efficient, clean, and nearly instantaneous. These are not utopian fantasies they are real possibilities that have been explored by visionaries throughout history. By embracing suppressed technologies, we can break free from the constraints of outdated systems and build a future that reflects our highest potential.

Unleashing Human Potential: Awakening the Extraordinary Abilities Within

Perhaps the most profound discovery of all is the untapped potential that lies within each of us. The psychic phenomena, superhuman abilities, and collective consciousness explored in this book are not just curiosities; they are windows into what it means to be fully human. For too long, we have been taught to see ourselves as separate, limited beings, disconnected from each other and the universe. But the truth is that we are far more powerful than we realize. Our minds can transcend space and time, our consciousness can influence the physical world, and our collective intent can shape reality.

Unlocking this potential requires a shift in how we view ourselves and our capabilities. It demands that we move beyond skepticism and embrace a spirit of exploration, experimentation, and openness. The abilities we have labeled as supernatural or paranormal are, in fact, natural extensions of our consciousness skills that can be developed, refined, and harnessed for the greater good. As we learn to trust our intuition, connect with our inner wisdom, and cultivate our latent talents, we can create lives filled with purpose, creativity, and joy.

Embracing the Unknown: The Courage to Question, Explore, and Evolve

The journey through the hidden secrets of humanity is not just an exploration of the past it is an invitation to shape the future. It calls us to question the narratives we have been told, to challenge the limitations imposed upon us, and to seek out the truth with courage and curiosity. This process is not always easy. It requires us to confront uncomfortable truths, to let go of old beliefs, and to embrace the mysteries that defy conventional understanding. But it is precisely in this space of uncertainty and wonder that the greatest breakthroughs occur.

Questioning Authority and Reclaiming Our Power

One of the key lessons of this journey is the importance of questioning authority. Whether it is the suppression of scientific discoveries, the distortion of historical narratives, or the manipulation of public perception, we have seen how those in power often seek to control information to maintain their dominance. But true knowledge cannot be contained forever. By cultivating critical thinking, independent research, and open dialogue, we can reclaim our power as seekers of truth and creators of our own destiny.

The democratization of information through the internet, citizen science, and alternative media has empowered individuals to challenge the official stories and explore new perspectives. This grassroots movement is a testament to the resilience of the human spirit and our unyielding drive to understand the world. It reminds us that knowledge is not the exclusive domain of experts or institutions it is the birthright of every person.

Exploring the Frontiers of Science and Spirituality

The convergence of science and spirituality is one of the most exciting developments of our time. As quantum physics, neuroscience, and consciousness studies continue to push the boundaries of what we know, they are revealing insights that echo the teachings of ancient mystics, shamans, and sages. The idea that reality is not fixed but fluid, that consciousness plays a central role in the universe, and that everything is interconnected are not just spiritual concepts they are scientific principles that challenge our most fundamental assumptions.

This merging of disciplines invites us to approach the mysteries of existence with an open mind and a sense of wonder. It encourages us to see the world not as a cold, mechanical construct but as a vibrant, living system where matter, energy, and mind are intertwined. By bridging the gap between science and spirituality, we can develop a more holistic understanding of the universe one that honors both the material and the metaphysical, the known and the unknown.

Evolving Together: The Power of Collective Consciousness

Our journey has also highlighted the profound impact of collective consciousness the idea that we are all connected through a shared field of awareness that influences the world around us. This concept is not just theoretical; it has practical implications for how we live, work, and interact with each other. When we come together with shared intent, whether through meditation, activism, or community-building, we create powerful ripples that can bring about real change.

The global challenges we face climate change, social inequality, political polarization are not insurmountable. They are symptoms of a deeper disconnection that can be healed through unity, empathy, and collaboration. By tapping into the power of collective consciousness, we can transcend the divisions that separate us and co-create a future that reflects our highest ideals. We are not powerless in the face of adversity; we are the architects of a new reality.

A Vision for the Future: Co-Creating a World of Possibility

As we look ahead, the vision of a transformed world a world where suppressed knowledge is brought to light, where human potential is fully realized, and where we live in harmony with each other and the cosmos feels not only possible but inevitable. This vision is not a distant dream; it is a call to action that begins with each of us. By embracing the hidden secrets of humanity, we can reclaim our rightful place as conscious creators and stewards of the Earth.

Building a Society That Honors Wisdom, Innovation, and Compassion

Imagine a society where education fosters curiosity and critical thinking, where scientific research is guided by ethics and the pursuit of the common good, and where spirituality is celebrated as a personal journey rather than a dogmatic institution. This is a society that values wisdom, nurtures creativity, and prioritizes the well-being of all its members. It is a place where ancient knowledge and modern innovation coexist, where sustainable technologies provide abundance without exploitation, and where every individual is empowered to explore their unique gifts.

Living in Harmony with the Earth and the Cosmos

The recognition that we are part of a conscious, living universe calls us to live in harmony with the natural world. This means not only protecting our environment but actively participating in its regeneration. Sustainable agriculture, renewable energy, and circular economies are not just solutions to environmental problems they are expressions of a deeper respect for the planet that sustains us. By aligning our actions with the rhythms of nature, we can create a world where prosperity and ecological balance go hand in hand.

Awakening to Our Cosmic Identity

Finally, our exploration of the cosmos has shown us that we are not alone. We are part of a vast, interconnected web of life that extends far beyond our planet. Whether through the potential for extraterrestrial contact, the mysteries of quantum entanglement, or the spiritual teachings of oneness, we are being invited to see ourselves as citizens of the universe. This cosmic identity transcends borders, cultures, and ideologies, reminding us that we are all connected by a shared destiny.

Embracing the Mystery: The Endless Journey of Discovery

The conclusion of this book is not an ending but a new beginning. The hidden secrets of humanity are an invitation to embark on an endless journey of discovery a journey that challenges us to look beyond the surface, to question what we think we know, and to embrace the mysteries that make life so extraordinary. It is a call to awaken to our true potential, to honor the wisdom of the past, and to co-create a future that reflects the best of who we are.

As we continue this journey, let us remember that the greatest secret of all is the power we hold within ourselves. The answers we seek are not hidden in some distant place; they are found in the choices we make, the actions we take, and the courage we summon to explore the unknown. Together, we can unlock the forbidden secrets of humanity and step into a future filled with infinite possibilities.

"The universe is not outside of you. Look inside yourself; everything that you want, you already are."
Rumi

Reflection Questions:

What hidden knowledge has most resonated with you, and how can you incorporate these insights into your daily life?

How can you contribute to the collective awakening and the co-creation of a more enlightened and harmonious

world?

What steps will you take to explore your own potential, question the status quo, and embrace the mysteries that connect us all?

Practical Steps Forward

As you reflect on the themes presented in this book, consider how you might integrate them into your life:

Stay Curious: Continue exploring topics that intrigue you. Read widely, engage in discussions, and seek experiences that expand your understanding.

Cultivate Mindfulness: Practice being present. Mindfulness enhances self-awareness and deepens your connection to others and the world.

Embrace Community: Connect with like-minded individuals. Shared journeys enrich personal growth and amplify collective impact.

Act with Integrity: Align your actions with your values. Integrity builds trust and fosters positive change.

Nurture Compassion: Extend kindness to yourself and others. Compassion heals divisions and strengthens bonds.

Advocate for Truth: Support transparency, ethical practices, and the free exchange of ideas.

Honor the Earth: Adopt sustainable practices and advocate for environmental stewardship.

Imagine Possibilities: Allow yourself to envision a future that reflects the highest potentials of humanity. Let this vision guide your choices.

A SHARED DESTINY

The challenges facing humanity are significant, but so are the opportunities. By embracing hidden knowledge and unlocking our collective potential, we can address global issues with wisdom and creativity. We can move beyond cycles of conflict and scarcity toward a future characterized by collaboration, abundance, and harmony.

This transformation requires each of us to play a part. No contribution is too small, every effort counts. As we awaken individually, we contribute to the awakening of humanity as a whole.

Gratitude And Hope

Thank you for embarking on this journey. Your willingness to explore, question, and reflect is a testament to the innate human desire for growth and understanding.

May the insights gained inspire you to live more fully, love more deeply, and contribute to a world where the forbidden secrets of humanity are no longer hidden but celebrated as the shared heritage of all.

"We are the music-makers,
And we are the dreamers of dreams,
Wandering by lone sea-breakers,
And sitting by desolate streams;
World-losers and world-forsakers,
On whom the pale moon gleams:
Yet we are the movers and shakers
Of the world forever, it seems."

Arthur O'Shaughnessy

Thank you for joining this exploration of the Forbidden Secrets of Humanity. May the insights and wisdom gained inspire you to live with purpose, seek truth, and embrace the extraordinary potential within us all.

Made in the USA
Columbia, SC
24 October 2024

43514454R00170